{Catchy Title Here}

{Catchy Title Here}

A Marke-Busi-Leade-Vation Book

30 Micro-courses on

Marketing, Business, Leadership and Motivation
based on the principles of Behavioral Economics

CHRIS MORIARITY

ISBN: 978-0-9997863-2-1

CONTENTS

DEDICATION AND ACKNOWLEDGEMENTS

My life can best be described as a "borrowed ladder." I've gained access to so much, completely due to the efforts of others. I spend a lot of time wondering if the things I share are actually helping anyone, and I wanted to put together a list of people that need never wonder.

Please don't be offended if you're not on this list; it doesn't mean you didn't have impact, it just means I ran out of beer.

Dedication(s)

I dedicate this book to the late Robert Bowers. His love of books was only surpassed by his love for his family, a family I am grateful to be part of. Miss you every day.

To my wife Laura and kids Presley, Cohen, and Brecken.

To my parents Pat and Peggy Moriarity.

To my sister Emily and her husband Malachi and their kids.

To my dogs Fancy Pants and Charlie.

Educators

Ann Visser
Laura Bremh
Mark Core
Dr. Amelia Demitrova
Dale Barnhill
Karl Korver
Greg Renaud

Mentors

Vicki McManus
Dr. Bruce Baird
Dr. Kim Kutsch
Bobby Bowers
Todd Markulics
Dan and Marcy Isdaner
Regan Robertson
Patti Sooy
Pete Peterson
Toni Bowers
Matt Giles
Jay Dering
Bob Cantrell
Ray Saluka
Micki Silvestri
Carrie Cady

Education

University of Northern Iowa
University of Illinois—IMBA program.

Friends

Cameron Keske
Curtis Lehmkuhl
Brent Shepard
Jesse and Jodi Droesch
Cody and Katie Clark
Dr. Carson and Haley Kutsch
Cynthia Baird
Cory Bowers
Jaxine Corum
Kendall and Garland Perry
Dr. Jonathan and Jodi Shafer
Brian and Jennifer Tottenham
John and Jessica Bowers
Cory "Hubba Hubba" Bowers

My Road Crew

Robbie Warren
Jennifer Hinsley
Monee Johnson
Heather Schuyler
Callie Ward
Christine Uhen
Jenni Bollman
Robyn Ramirez
Tennli Toole
Deidre Bently
Kelly Bellinger
Angela Sullivan
Sommer Carol
Brenda Barbour
Kathryn Gilliam

Moriarity Clan

Gerald Moriarity who inspired my love for the written word.
Betty, with her positive mental attitude.
Patrick and Peggy Moriarity for their love and support.
Moriarity Aunts, Uncles, In-laws, outlaws, and cousins.
Lee Roy Proctor, for his work ethic, and his companion.
Carol for her caring heart.
Rosemary Hugen for her love and support.
Danette and Clark Peterson, for their love of life!

INTRODUCTION

Look at your practice. It's good, but is it the best it could be? If you're in a field like dentistry, ophthalmology, cosmetic surgery, or chiropractic, you don't depend on insurers and HMOs to send you patients and bankroll procedures. It can be a struggle to not rely on insurance, since many of your patients are coming from a mindset of just paying the co-pay and letting insurance pay the rest. Not relying on insurance is also a great opportunity. Freed from the shackles of pre-approval and limits on care, you can increase your productivity, attract new patients, and help people create real, positive change in their lives.

I wrote this book for one simple reason. I get calls from offices all day long. These offices have somehow come to believe that success isn't possible due to the team they have, the location they are in, the insurance they take, and so on.

If I analyze ten offices a week, six of them are scared to death. They can't pay their taxes; they can't make payroll; and forget about taking home a paycheck. Two of the offices are probably startups. They're typically $1 million in debt and they will literally do whatever you tell them, even if it's the worst advice possible. The last two offices are hyper-achievers. These offices are going 80 miles an hour, but they want to know how they can go 100 miles an hour without the wheels falling off.

The first six are fun to help; who doesn't like a good comeback story? The second two are satisfying, but it's the last two where all the lessons are learned. These hyper-achieving offices are located in literally every demographic you can think of. Small towns, big cities, PPOs, fee-for-service, you name it. So what makes them different? What are the things they are doing that anyone could do?

Now I'm not saying that there aren't circumstances that may prevent success; if you have an office in middle-of-nowhere Pennsylvania that depends on a coal mine and that coal mine shuts down, that's going to be a problem. However, I can't imagine that's many of you. If you live in an area that makes you say, "People here don't need much dentistry/eye care/cosmetic surgery/whatever else I offer," then move to a place where people do. Or, maybe, just maybe, there are people who need you, but they don't know how to find you.

Everyone deserves to be successful. I don't care if you are a solo doc operation, a group practice, or corporately owned. I have seen every model succeed, and I have seen every model fail. The number one question I get is "What do the hyper-achievers have that I don't?" The short answer is nothing. The long answer involves the simple concept of being uncomfortable.

Take a second and imagine yourself in the most comfortable position possible. This could be a hammock on a beach, a giant feather bed, or whatever comes to mind. Now as you sit and sink into this comfortable place, what's going to happen to you? Absolutely nothing. Growth typically doesn't come from being comfortable. It comes from pushing the boundaries. It comes from learning new skills, learning new ways to communicate, and learning more successful ways to lead. Whoever can stand being uncomfortable for the longest period of time wins. Those who are comfortable get lazy, and lazy people don't grow.

If you aren't growing, you're dying.

Does that sound extreme? Too bad, because it's absolute reality. Nothing around you is getting cheaper. Rent goes up, supply costs go up, and I'm guessing you'd like to make more money next year than you did this year. Even if you don't, I can guarantee you that your team does.

Albert Einstein once said that if you can't explain something simply then you must not fully understand it. The guidance and recommendations in this book are designed to be simple. As the expression goes, this isn't rocket science. (Side note: I actually met a genuine rocket scientist once and I had to ask if they use that expression. He said they didn't; they say, "It's not like talking to girls!")

These 30 micro-courses are based on my years of experience in dental and medical consulting. Every day, I take small practices and turn them into some of the most productive in the country. My clients can achieve work-life balance, teach others, and live passionately, doing good while doing well. Now, I'm sharing my experiences with you. Any independent medical practice can use these tools to increase productivity and become a truly great place to visit and to work.

So, get ready to embark on a month that changes your life. With one short course a day, you can have the practice you always wanted, a practice that grows, a practice that is super-productive.

COURSE 1

How Playing Monopoly Can Teach You to Expand Your Reach

How many of you have ever played Monopoly? What happens when you pass Go? You collect $200. Why?

This is where things get interesting. Most people have played Monopoly dozens of times over the course of their life and the vast majority of them couldn't tell you why you get the $200 just for making it around the board. It's the rules of the game. It doesn't mean anything. It's random, like everything else that turns on the roll of a dice.

Grab your Monopoly board right now and take a look at the Go square. You'll see the answer to my question printed in plain English. "Collect $200 salary as you pass Go." That's right, the $200 is actually your salary. This poses a very interesting question. Have you ever heard of anybody winning the game of Monopoly simply by passing Go the most times? Of course not! I can't imagine how that would even be possible, even if the player rolled 12-12-11 on every single turn.

So, what is this game? On its most basic level, Monopoly is a real estate investment game. But let's just call it an investment game. Naturally, offices that invest in their future success tend to do better than offices who are focused on the present.

To be clear, this is not limited to clinical development. In fact, the clinical development seems to be the easy part. Turns out, most practitioners like to learn new things about their field. What a shock! Many of us hold the firm belief that if we could just become the world's best clinician, patients would flock to our doors. Sadly, often this isn't the case.

In fact, there seems to be an inverse correlation between the number of letters behind a doctor's name and their production. These multi-boarded, multi-certified practitioners are the most frustrated people on the planet. They spend years watching C-students enjoy full parking lots, while they struggle with empty slots in the schedule. The only joy they seem to experience is when they get to present a case to the local study club where they fixed some other "idiot's" work. It's not a very good consolation prize, when the idiot is making money hand over fist and just bought a vacation cottage in Aspen.

So, back to Monopoly. Salary alone won't get you ahead. It produces stagnation. It's a death trap for your practice. Investing in CE is important, but it can't be your only strategy. People don't win Monopoly based on salary alone, but they also don't win just by collecting the waterworks and the electric company and then waiting for people to land on them again and again.

What works in Monopoly? And how do these tactics relate to transforming your practice?

Monopoly experts Craig Way and Ken Koury gave readers of

Thrillest a primer on how to become a monopoly expert. Here are some of their best hints, and what they mean for you.

Tip #1: Never be the banker. Koury and Way explain that the banker can become distracted making change and lose sight of bigger strategic issues, crippling their Monopoly game as other players triumph.

What this Means for Your Practice: Outsource or insource what you can, especially mundane or repetitive tasks. Don't micromanage. Having good business managers, marketing teams, clinical assistants, and facilities personnel lets you focus on building your business. And the practice is a business.

Tip #2: Buy every property you land on. Buying properties makes it easier to get natural monopolies and shuts out your competition.

What this Means for Your Practice: Take advantage of opportunities to learn new skills, enter new markets, or test new technologies. Being the first, or only, person in your area to do something gives you a boost among prospective patients. This also applies to case presentation. No, you can't close every case. But you need to give every case your best shot.

Tip #3: Oranges get landed on the most. Buy them. Analyzing the cards in the game, patterns of dice rolls, and ROI suggests that orange properties give you the most bang for your pastel-colored buck.

What this Means for Your Practice: Learn to collect the numbers and analyze the numbers. Your decisions for marketing, hiring, fees, and new procedures should be rooted in data. Too many of us want to trust our instincts or our guts when expanding our practices, but that's not how you become super-productive. Get the data, analyze the data, and act on the data.

Tip #4: Buy as many houses as you can, as quickly as you can. Don't bother with hotels. In Monopoly, houses are a limited resource. Once they're gone, they're gone. Controlling access to the houses helps you win the game. Hotels don't help you get ahead, because by putting houses back into play, they let your competitors catch up with you.

What this Means for Your Practice: What are the limited resources in your area? Often, it's great employees or prime real estate. What can you do to hire and retain great employees? How can you buy up great real estate or build connections with high-profile local employers? Look for limited resources and find out how you can use them.

Tip #5: Don't be a jerk. Since monopoly is a game of trading and dealmaking, you can't win by being a jerk. Or you can, but it will be ugly and no one will ever agree to play with you again. At the end of the day, relationships matter more than dice rolls or scheming.

What this Means for Your Practice: What they said. Don't be a jerk. A successful practice needs a happy team and happy patients. Learn to build strong relationships; be the practitioner whom everyone loves. You'll have a more experienced and skilled team, happier patients, and a better place in your community.

In later micro-courses, I'll expand on how to achieve these goals, but for now, here are the questions to ask yourself:

- What tasks have I outsourced?
- What tasks have I insourced?

- What am I doing that someone else could do nearly as well?
- Where do I tend to micromanage?
- What new skills have I learned this year?
- What new marketing tactics have I tried this year?
- How have I improved my case presentation in the last year?
- How am I using data to improve my practice?
- What data do I wish I could collect?
- What is my plan to collect that data?
- How am I working to recruit top employees?
- What am I doing to keep the employees I have?
- Do I keep an eye out for new markets or business connections?
- Do my team members and patients like me?
- Do other medical professionals in my area like me?
- What can I do to be friendlier and more valuable to my community?

Congratulations. If you've answered all of these questions, you have a pretty good idea of some steps you can take to transform your practice into a hyper-achieving one. Now, look at your list. Pick one action item and get to work. It's the first movement in a month of transformation.

Chapter Sources

1 *https://www.thrillist.com/entertainment/nation/how-to-win-at-monopoly-every-time-according-to-experts*

COURSE 2

Cultivation Theory

Look around your life and your practice. Is it what you expected when you were 18, or maybe 22, and deciding on your career? Do you constantly find yourself looking at what is and growing angry about the huge gap between what *is* and what *should be*? If your practice or your family is objectively in crisis, this reaction makes sense. But for most people in our field, the problem isn't that the family or the practice is failing. It's that we're working from a false idea of what real life is like.

If that's your problem, you're not delusional. You've just fallen prey to Cultivation Theory. Cultivation Theory describes how our exposure to images in the media affects our view of reality. Over a lifetime the fictions presented by television and social media take a toll on our minds. When you were a child or teenager, did you watch any shows involving doctors or dentists? The life looked pretty glamorous, right? Practicing medicine was a perfect blend of fascinating cases, fast cars, and sexy coworkers. Then everyone went home to adoring spouses and precious, precocious children. If you're on social media, some of your former classmates may even seem to be living this life now. We all know that guy who posts weekly shots of himself with his Tesla at sunset on some California beach.

Meanwhile, what's your reality? Most cases are routine; you drive the speed limit to avoid tickets; your car is a nice SUV that's practical for taking the Cub Scouts on hikes; your coworkers are all normal people; and when you come home, your kids are whining about homework and asking for screen time while you and your spouse try to plan who is driving which child where at which time tomorrow and the frozen pizza cooks in the oven. In other words, you live a totally normal American upper-middle-class life, and you have not yet figured out how to replace your children with robots. But it feels like a second-rate life because decades of media exposure have left you expecting something different. You're like the two-year-old who cries at the zoo because the animals don't talk like they do on cartoons. Reality isn't broken. Your expectations are broken.

If false expectations are unavoidable for those of us raised on a steady diet of media from the time we were toddlers, how can you stop living in a fantasy world and learn to love your life? Talk to people in the same field. The best antidote to fantasy is reality. When we share our struggles with other people, we learn that our struggles aren't unique. Everyone is in the same boat. No one is living the Dr. McDreamy life. Everyone has days where they're bored; where the kids drive them crazy; where they want to chuck it all, buy an RV, and see America instead of patients. Maybe our field needs the equivalent to Mommy bloggers—people who tell the truth and keep it real, within HIPPA guidelines, of course, so that the rest of us can learn that we're not failures, we're human.

Recalibrating your sense of reality can take a bit of time. Here are some steps you can take to speed up the process:

1. Join a local professional group. Meet other people who own practices, and swap stories. Brainstorm, ask questions, and get perspective.

2. Talk about your kids more, and listen to what other people say about theirs. Chances are, your kids aren't abnormally defiant or ill-behaved.

3. Coach your kids' teams, lead their scout troops, or volunteer at Sunday school. Get perspective and help youth in your community at the same time.

4. Every night, take time to catalogue what went right in your practice or family that day. Stop focusing on what Joe with the Tesla must be doing right, and celebrate your own success.

5. Spend more time in national and state parks. Getting out into nature will remind you how lucky you are and how great the world is. Set a goal for two hours a week enjoying somewhere beautiful, then gradually increase it.

COURSE 3

Stop Being an Octopus, Start Being Yourself

The octopus is known for many things. One of those things is the ability to camouflage. I'm pretty sure the only creature capable of better camouflage than an octopus is a practice owner. Many times someone reaches out to our team and says he needs more money. He wants us to help him increase productivity and production so that he can have more cash on hand. But, as I talk to him, I discover that the reality is he just needs more time, better leadership, less stress, more respect, or even simply to feel valued for what he does. Money typically doesn't make the top five concerns, once we really start talking to someone. So, how about you? You may be camouflaging yourself as someone who's in your field for the flashy cars and big houses, but what really gets you up and out of bed in the morning?

The following exercise is designed to break down your camouflage and help you discover your true motivations for running your practice, building your business, and living your life. Yes, it's based on an internet personality quiz that's been circulating since the 1990s. However, it still gives you a bit of insight into what things about your practice are bogging you down and sapping your joy.

Write down the animal words: cow, tiger, sheep, horse, and pig. Now rank them 1 to 5, quickly, without thinking. The different animals represent different concepts that are important to your self-identity. Now, which one did you rank first?

Did You Choose Cow?

The Cow represents career. To be happy, you need to feel like you're learning, growing, and constantly improving. If you chose cow and are unhappy with your practice, it's probably because you feel bored, trapped, and stunted.

It's easy to fall into a routine, doing the same procedures over and over. You're really good at them, the patients need them, and you're making a decent living. You may think more production and more collections will give you more freedom to do what you want, but what you really want is professional growth.

So, learn to delegate a little. Find out what tasks you can delegate to assistants—this varies considerably by state—or junior associates, and spin them off. Now think about something you've always wished you could do. Do you want to improve your business skills and management acumen? Maybe you should find time to work towards an MBA. Is there a new therapy or procedure you're fascinated with? Sign up for continuing education and learn it. Production and collections will increase as you learn new skills and improve your outlook on the practice. Do what it takes to make your career interesting and joyful again, instead of days of drudge work.

Did You Choose Tiger?

In most dental and medical groups, Tiger is the top choice, and usually by a large margin. The image and the idea of the Tiger are most closely associated with the concept of pride. It's no surprise that this is a top choice in our industry. Clinical excellence is incredibly difficult to achieve and requires a rare degree of skill.

The average patient has no idea what it takes to do what you do. After all, you make it look easy. They walk in assuming that you'll be able to heal them and won't kill or maim them in the process. After all, you have letters after your name! They can't really observe you at work, and, in any case, they don't have the training to realize how hard you had to work to learn and master the skills of your specialty.

Many practitioners feel incredibly isolated because nobody can appreciate what they do. Patients don't notice how careful you are, how even small mistakes could wound them, how you've practiced and trained so that you're an expert in your field, just as Payton Manning was an expert in his. No, they don't appreciate your skill, hard work, and talent, but they always notice the price. When they try to haggle with you like you're a used car dealer, it hurts your pride.

If you chose the Tiger, your dissatisfaction with your practice isn't really about wanting to make more money, except in the sense that higher collections mean people value you more. What you really want is appreciation and recognition. You want authority. You want your patients to trust you and look up to you.

Did You Choose Sheep?

Have you ever heard the old saying, "It is better to be feared than loved?" Not if you're a sheep. You're unhappy with your practice because you value human connections. You want to feel like you're changing lives, helping people, and building real, personal relations with your patients and team.

You've lost the joy in your practice because you've become too focused on lists, schedules, and reports. These are all important, but they need to support your goals, not become the goals themselves. So, how can you reinvigorate your practice and keep growing? Reorient on people.

Relax your schedule a bit, so you have time to really talk to and—more importantly—listen to each patient. Schedule regular team-building days, where you can all enjoy each other's company away from the office. And, most of all, look for new people to serve, people who really need what you can offer, people whose lives you can change.

For instance, one noted cosmetic surgeon takes several weeks off a year to go on mission trips to the developing world. While he enjoys helping his stateside patients achieve their beauty goals, what really feeds his spirit and keeps him motivated is these trips abroad, where he can help people whose injuries or congenital deformities have kept them from getting an education, having a job, or building a family. He values love and service, and he looks forward to finding and helping the people that only he can help.

Many dentists run annual free clinics, where they provide services to people without dental insurance. Often these patients are in tremendous amounts of pain and have given up any hope of ever having a healthy mouth. These life-changing clinics help remind us why we got into dentistry in the first place, and what a beautiful gift a healthy mouth can be.

Look around you. No matter what your specialty, there is someone in the world who needs your blend of skills. You can change lives. Reorient your practice, and you'll recover your joy and grow as a result.

Did You Choose Horse?

Horse means that the good of your family is your prime motivator. If you're unhappy with your practice and chose horse, you may feel like your career is keeping you away from your family. Maybe you worked hard to build your practice when your children were young, but now you want to be able to make camp-outs and ball games. Maybe changes in the business of running a practice have ruined your work-life balance. Are you bringing too much paperwork home? Do you want to travel to see aging parents or new grandchildren, but you feel tied down by your responsibilities?

If you chose horse, your unhappiness is less about money than it is about scheduling and efficiency. Perhaps you're thinking that if your collections were higher, you could bring in an associate and then have more time off. But who's going to want to buy into a practice where everyone is miserable? To have the sort of practice that gives you the freedom to hire an associate, you first need to get a handle on scheduling, collections, and administrative details.

Any Pigs Out There?

Interestingly enough, pig tends to be the least selected option or the lowest ranked. Pig is the image and idea that is most closely linked to money. And yet it is routinely the lowest on the totem pole. Now don't get me wrong, money is very important, but these exercises simply highlight that it tends not to be our primary motivator.

It does, however, tend to be a primary stressor. It's important that we understand the distinction between a motivator and a stressor. Money can certainly give you more freedom of choice, but it rarely leads to satisfaction or a sense of overall well-being. Granted—if you can't pay the rent, very little else matters. But once we achieve financial stability, we need to ensure that we're not chasing our tails thinking more and more money is going to make us happier and happier. It's not. What will make you happy is finding out what motivates you, and restructuring your practice so that you can grow, recover your joy, and have your number one motivator as your number one priority.

COURSE 4

How Your Favorite Barista Can Transform Your Team

"People just don't want to work anymore."

"Millennials are lazy and entitled."

"I'd like to expand, but there aren't enough people who want to be hired."

It's true that the economy is approaching full or nearly full employment, but that doesn't mean you can't find great people for your team. After all, you're running a successful medical practice. It's a growth industry, your working conditions are fairly pleasant, and you give employees chances to develop their skills. But you're not going to find your new star employee at a career fair, or in your competitor's office. To make great hires, check out your local coffee shop.

Good Employees Hire Good Employees

It's inefficient to try to hire staff from other offices. If they're a good employee, they're probably happy where they're at. Yes, they may have all their certifications in place, but certifications are attainable. Skills are learnable. Someone who's happy in their current position is going to require a huge investment of time and money to recruit.

The reality is that almost everything support staff does is trainable and coachable. It's a lot harder to teach the soft skills: ambition, conscientiousness, and the desire to do one's best even when there's no supervisor present.

The first key to great hiring is to have your current team members select and train your new team members. If someone isn't working out, your team should handle the firing. If you don't trust your team to make these decisions, you should hold off on hiring new staff until you've got your current staff to a level where they understand your practice philosophy and can train and correct each other without constant input from you.

Poach the Best from Another Field

So where do you find new employees that your team will love? It's time to ditch want-ads, craigslist, and job fairs. Instead, you're going to go hunting in some of the harshest environments known to man. These places force people to think quickly, prioritize accuracy, be kind under pressure, and keep going even when they're exhausted. These environments are hot, loud, fast-paced bubbles where the customer is always right and frequently rude. They put new employees through the meat grinder, so that only the best survive. From the employees' perspective, their jobs may well be the closest thing to purgatory you'll find on Earth. If it wasn't for the caffeine, no one would survive.

Yes. I am talking about your friendly neighborhood coffee shop.

Give your team $100, and have them get up at the crack of dawn and try out area coffee shops. Make complicated orders. Give hard to pronounce names. See which baristas take amazing care of you and leave you feeling cherished and satisfied. That's who you want. Someone who wakes up at 4 am, works for minimum wage, and still manages to send customers away with a spring in their step, ready to face their own work day. Go back every day for a week and see who remembers your name and your go-to drink. These people are the employees you want. **They're hardworking and service-minded and go beyond their job descriptions.**

Retail workers also make great additions to your office team, for the same reasons. Look for someone in a thankless, high-pressure, commission-based sales job where the top producers thrive and everyone else lasts less than 90 days. Let Nordstrom and Victoria's Secret do the vetting for you. We're not looking for high-pressure sales people, but we are looking for people that can connect with a stranger in less than a minute and find a way to take care of them. You need to hire these people.

"*But what do I say?*" you're yelling. Just keep reading. I'm going to give you a quick lesson in how to leave someone dying to work for your practice.

Positioning

Here's how you're going to start the conversation:

"Can I ask you a quick question?
How did you get so good at your job?"

This is called a pattern-interrupt. It'll catch them off guard, and in these low-praise jobs, they may not even have a prepared answer for you. Listen to what they say, and it'll usually boil down to treating people how they'd like to be treated. Perfect.

"The reason I ask is that I own an <insert specialty> *practice and I made a commitment from Day 1 that my patients deserve the best. Your job is tough, and I've watched you take amazing care of people. I'd love to talk to you about joining my team. Don't worry about the medical stuff, we can teach you that. What I can't teach is attitude, and yours is perfect."*

Take out two business cards, have them jot their info for you on one, and give them the other. These words are chosen specifically and are designed to simultaneously demonstrate your leadership and character while explaining the expectations of an employee. An employee for us is someone who has a great attitude and takes amazing care of people. We can teach you the rest. Simple.

Practice your script until you can make these sudden job offers smoothly and confidently. This should be a 60-second conversation, maximum. Bait the hook, then get out. Less is more. By witnessing this candidate in the real world, you virtually eliminate the issue of meeting a candidate's "interview self." I need to know who you are when you are under pressure, tired, and ideally dealing with difficult people.

Answering the Big Question, In and Out of Interviews

Too many people fall into the trap of thinking that candidates need to know the job title, job description, and hiring range. That's why most employment advertisements read like clones of each other. I could pull 10 random interviews from Indeed, and if I stripped out the job title and industry specific certifications, you'd probably think they were all for the same position at the same firm. **Generic advertisements attract generic candidates.** And you're not a generic practice, because if you were, you'd be going out of business, not looking to expand.

What your candidates really need to know is, "Why this job?"

If I were to ask you what a dental or medical assistant does, how would you answer that? Most people would list off the functions of the job. When the day is laid out in minute detail, the job sounds dull. Grueling. Awful. Instead, explain what your office does. How does the position you're hiring for help change lives and make the world a better place?

> *"99% of my patients are pretty nervous when they come see us. I rely on my assistants to be the cornerstone of the entire relationship. You'll be amazed how much patients will rely on you. They'll ask your advice and you'll find a way to get them healthy. We've had patients in here that haven't smiled in a picture in 60 years and we make that happen. You have no idea how that feels."*

Suddenly, I don't want to serve coffee anymore. I want people to rely on me and I want to give people smiles. Don't you?

Paying Your New Team Members

Yes, this is important. But it's not the most important. We've done a wonderful job creating a generation of medical office mercenaries. They're always seeking another dollar-per-hour, moving office to office, and working for the highest bidder. It's not good for our industry, our offices, or our patients.

I don't need a 22-year-old who demands 13 weeks off. I'll take the single mother of 3, grinding out the midnight to eight shift at Denny's on Christmas Eve. She knows everyone's name, they know hers, and they love her. That's who I want. You hire her, invest in her education, and restore her health, and you'll have a soldier for life, I can promise you that.

The biggest challenge in recruiting isn't the pay. It's that we try to attract the people that no longer get amazed by the impact we have. Break the mold. Shake some hands. Be different and never forget what you really do.

And never leave home without a card in your pocket. You never know where you'll meet your next great employee.

COURSE 5

All I Know About Case Presentation, I Learned from High School English Class

Most dental and medical practices tend to be fairly systematic and lend themselves well to scale. If one doc can run 3 ops, then two can run 6; three can run 9; and so on. We can just replicate each bundle on into infinity, provided we have a few constants that keep up on the way.

Ah, that feels nice. Predictability feels nice. So, why do most things feel so unpredictable?

It's because you work with humans, and deep down you're still human too.

In business, we're always looking for trends. If we do *X* and that results in *Y*, then if we do *10X* we'll have *10Y,* and if we do *100X*... On the clinical side, we know how to do this. You can do a given procedure in *X* minutes. You can turn a room in *X* minutes. The problem is that while we can scale up clinical and support skills, it's very difficult to scale up soft skills.

Take case presentation. Case presentation is basically a sales talk. We're trying to convince our patients that we have a product that will solve their problems, and that our product is a fair price for the benefits it provides. The problem is that people aren't as predictable as procedures. When it comes to buying behavior, people are all over the place. Some people just want the facts; others want feelings. Some need the details and others will run screaming from the details. You don't have time to throw darts until you figure out what the patient needs to hear. You need a communication system that takes you down a path that leads to patient understanding and a crystal-clear next step.

A good communication system helps increase case acceptance. Not because a script persuades patients, but because a system makes it easier for your team to support you. If you get distracted or derailed, a system can let your staff step in and help you get back on track. If you're always in improv mode, on the other hand, your team can't tell when you need help, and when you're just riffing off a prompt.

I like to call this communication system the "One-Act Play." We built a communication system that walks the patient through their dental needs and ultimately adds context to the treatment plan without beating them to death with science. Like a good one-act play, the system includes an introduction of the main players, an introduction to the problem, escalating tension, a satisfying release, and then a denouement.

Your ninth grade English teacher would be able to look at this system and see where we were going. Why do we use a One-Act Play? Because it works. People are hardwired to look for stories. Stories are how we understand the world. A good story is instantly more compelling than a random series of facts, which is why everything—from the nightly news to the fund-raising brochures you get in the mail at Christmas—focuses on these common plot elements. Now don't you feel bad for telling Mrs. Jones you were never going to use any of this Drama stuff in the real world?

A One-Act Medical Drama Case Presentation Made Easy

So, how do you organize your case presentation into a gripping medical drama? The key is to break it down into parts of a story.

- **Step 1: The cast of characters.** For your case presentation, the cast of characters are the patient's risk factors. For instance, a dentist discussing caries treatments and scaling might talk about a history of past decay and failed restorations, issues with the gums, and systemic health issues like diabetes and heart disease. An ophthalmologist recommending corrective surgery might talk about the current state of the patient's vision, what activities are ill-suited to corrective lenses, and why the current time period was ideal for corrective surgery.
- **Step 2: The Problem/Dramatic Tension.** The next act in the play is to set up the problem. "The risk factors are leading towards *X* conclusion if you choose to do nothing." Ideally, you should present the problem in the form of a story. "If you do nothing, first <event> will happen. As time goes on, <event> and <event> are likely to follow. By not addressing these risk factors, you will eventually have <problem> and have to suffer <consequences> and pay <amount> to correct it."
- **Step 3: The Climax.** Just as it looks like the future is hopeless, the solution is presented. "To prevent these consequences, we can offer you this service/procedure."

- **Step 4: Resolution and Denouement.** This is where you explain outcomes, scheduling, and pricing; answer any questions; and, in many cases, schedule the procedure.

It doesn't matter what your specialty is, a good one-act drama can help you present cases effectively. Try it out with some of the situations you see frequently in your practice. Now, introduce the staff to the one-act drama. Once they know the script, they can act as that little guy who sits at the front of the stage, feeding you cues if you lose your place. "Doctor, if she doesn't address these risk factors, what's likely to happen?" "How soon can we get her in for the procedure?" Your team can help direct the drama, keeping you—the lead actor—on script and focused on the play.

When you take on the role of lead actor in a one-act play, you gain a level of predictability that can dramatically lower stress and increase production. We all know the cost of not doing this. You give the same patient to five different docs and we'll have five different outcomes from the case presentation. This is the bane of the multi-doc office, and oddly it's often the most clinically gifted that get beat up on the production numbers. It certainly doesn't have to be that way. You just need to create your One-Act Play, get out of your own way, and let your team back you up so that you can connect more patients with the procedures they need.

COURSE 6

GoPro and the Limits of Branding a Practice

Before I get started, I'm going to give you a simple mantra. I want you to repeat this, memorize this, and take it to heart: **You can't pay bills with branding.** Various marketing consultants will act like defining and solidifying your brand is a magic bullet. Just redo your logo, carry the color theme through all your materials and decorating, and you'll thrive.

Very few people get to truly pull back the curtain on the business side of a practice and evaluate a business from the top-line to the bottom-line. What you'd find is a virtual Bermuda Triangle of wealth. Money goes in the top, and most of it's just plain gone when you reach the bottom. Practice owners are in a constant state of keeping up with the Joneses. They'll spend money hand over fist for technology and gorgeous buildings, with little thought to the critical path that's going to keep them in the black and on the road to prosperity.

For the most part, those practices that you believe are crushing it are actually just spending it. It tends to be the folks in the middle that have the healthiest businesses.

It seems logical, except our emotions don't allow us to win the logic game. We still want to win the popularity game. We all want to be #1 when people think about the specialists in our area. But there can be only *one*! If you're spending money hand over fist to be number one, you're chasing an empty honor at the expense of your practice. It's not just you. We see this pattern across industries.

Look at GoPro. My guess is that most of the people reading this article own at least one of their devices. We see them everywhere. In every show, in every sport. I even saw one attached to a hawk once...it was incredible. These guys own action sports and high adventure. GoPro Inc. is so far into first place that there is no second.

So, riddle me this: On August 10th, 2015, Go Pro Inc. was trading at $65.49 a share. Less than a year later it was trading at $8.62 (May 19, 2016). Millions upon millions of dollars were erased in a matter of months. One of the most successfully branded items in history is now a financial leper. In fact, they recently posted an operating loss of $121.4 million.

How did this happen?

Without going down a numbers hole, here's what happened in a nutshell:

1. They shifted the new product base to try and attract the masses, but the smaller (but lower quality) cameras proved to be a flop.
2. They discounted. In an effort to salvage the failing new line of cameras, they dropped the price by $100, leaving almost

no meat on the bone. They assumed that the masses wanted the new camera, just not at the higher price point. They were wrong and were left with low sales and no margin.

3 They couldn't innovate soon enough. GoPro has been talking about their new drone Karma for far too long and production delays have worn out investors.

What does this mean for your practice? Look at who your patients are and where your money comes from. If you're a niche practice attracting high-quality patients, trying to become more popular may actually destroy your ability to pay the rent and make a profit.

It's not that branding is bad, necessarily, but being the guy on every billboard, the specialist whose name first comes to mind, is not really an effective way to build your practice. In our business, the business of specialty medical care, businesses don't really get built on big flashy buildings, fancy television campaigns, or big ads on the back of phone books.

Like the original GoPro, your best brand-builders are clinical excellence and good word of mouth. If Ellen wants to have her breasts redone or Jake wants cosmetic dentistry, they're not going to look for the guy on the billboard. They're going to ask a friend or acquaintance who's already had the procedure. And they're either going to hear, "Go to my doc, she's great!" or "Don't go to the guy I saw, he's terrible."

In the end, it's not how your business cards look, a memorable slogan, or hearing your voice on the radio every morning. It's how you run your practice.

- Do appointments usually run on schedule?
- Does your team radiate cheer and compassion?

- Do your patients like you?
- Are your operatories always clean and well organized?
- Is your billing department prompt, clear, and easy to deal with?
- What's the first impression every new patient has of your office?
- What's the impression you leave patients with when you release them from care?

Optimize your books and processes before jumping on a fantasy treadmill that will only leave you broke and tired. In the finance world we say, "Plan the trade and trade the plan." The only goals you need to worry about are yours. What's your plan? Are you on track? Are you protecting profits? GoPro tried to take over the world, and the branding succeeded, but the business hasn't. You can try and pay your bills in branding, but most of the banks still only accept dollars.

COURSE 7

Thinking about Buying or Selling a Practice? An Old Joke has an Important Lesson

You've probably heard this one before, but read it anyway. There's an important lesson in this story.

Three men on a road trip decide to grab a cheap hotel for the night. The price of the room is $30. In the morning, they each pitch in $10 ($10 x 3 = $30) and begin to leave. The manager stops them and explains that he overcharged them. The price of the room was supposed to be $25, so he hands them back five $1 bills ($25 + $5 = $30). Each man takes back $1, and they give the manager $2 as a tip for his honesty ($3 + $2 = $5).

So, with a dollar back, each man has now paid $9 towards the room, but here's where it gets odd. If each man paid $9, that's $27 ($9 x 3 = $27). Adding in the $2 tip, that only equals $29 ($27 + $2 = $29).

What happened to the missing dollar?

Now, obviously we're having a little fun here and it's pretty easy to solve the riddle after a bit, but I'm sure a few of you found yourselves scratching your heads a bit.

Buying and selling a practice in today's world is both easier and harder than ever. Information is simultaneously easier to access and easier to manipulate. If you've ever done any fundamental analysis of a company, what you'll learn is they're trying to tell a story with the numbers. That story is going to be biased almost 100% of the time. Redundancy and independent reports are crucial.

The biggest hurdle that we people with specialty medical practices need to overcome is the fact that we're very intelligent. We worked hard to learn math and science, to excel in high school and college, and to make it through our professional programs. We were used to being at the top of our classes, the smartest person in the room. Even in our professional programs, when we weren't the smartest in the room, it was because everyone in the room was far above average. We're used to being able to understand complex material and solving problems with our minds. This is great when we're in the operatory. It can be devastating when we start dealing with problems outside of our zone of competence.

Don't think you can be fooled? Remember Enron? The top CFAs, CPAs, mutual funds, hedge funds, and advisors all got taken, and it wasn't for a lack of due diligence. Now, obviously, this was a criminal matter, but it's not far from what we see happen in practice sales every day. This is especially true when it comes to the percentage of patients participating in insurance or Medicare programs. Without accurate information, a practice that looks great on paper may turn out to be barely staying afloat—or at least not worth as much as you're about to pay for it.

So, if you're buying a practice, what information beyond the big picture (collections, expenses, appraisals of property) do you need?

- Ask for the total number of patients who've been active *in the last year*, not the total number of patients. Many practices are lousy about purging the roles of inactive, or even dead, patients.
- Ask for the number of patients who bill Medicare, Anthem/ Blue Cross, Humana, etc. You need a breakdown not just of the number of insured patients, but also which insurers cover which percent of the practice? For instance, a practice where 90% of the existing active patients are covered by Anthem is going to be a practice that's essentially held hostage to Anthem.
- Ask for the number of cash pay patients, and the total collections received from—not billed to—this group. Cash pay patients who pay their bills are gold in any industry.
- Get the total stats on any in-house financing plans.
- Spend a day, or have an agent spend the day, sitting in the waiting room. What do you see? What do the patients seem like?
- Sit down and talk to the team. What do they see as the strengths of the practice? What do they see as the weaknesses?
- Look at the practice benefit structure and current staff. If necessary, get an actuary involved to make sure that the current levels are sustainable. No one is going to stick around for a new owner who comes in and immediately cuts benefits and pay to keep the office stable.

Take the time and spend the money to look at any and all numbers. Even if they simply confirm the original numbers, you'll sleep soundly knowing you've made the right investment.

On the flip side, if you're selling the practice, don't be like the jokester who invented the problem we started with. Be honest. Make it easy to find your numbers; be clear about what they represent. You'll get a better price if potential buyers don't feel like you're pulling a fast one by couching numbers in confusing stories. If you're unsure of how to present your practice for sale, hire help. You're brilliant, but that doesn't mean you're omnicompetent.

So, what if you're not planning on buying or selling a practice in the near future? Was this course a waste of time? Of course not! The same tactics you'd use to assess an unknown practice's fiscal health can be used to assess your own practice's health.

Run the numbers on yourself. Look at the story that emerges. If you were looking to buy a practice, would you buy yours? If not, what numbers need to change so that it would be a brilliant business opportunity instead of a millstone? Think of your practice like a patient. Until you run the tests and have an accurate diagnosis, you can't guide it to health.

COURSE 8

Use the Baader-Meinhof Principle to Expand Your Practice

Let me just start with a simple truth. The universe isn't conspiring for, or against, anyone. Successful practitioners aren't part of some chosen sect and struggling offices aren't hopeless.

You always hear, "Success is where preparation meets opportunity." Well, what happens when all you seem to be doing is preparing? Days turn into month, months into years, and you find yourself very prepared for opportunities that never seem to come.

Why are you missing the opportunities? Why is your practice stagnant, when those of your colleagues seem to be experiencing steady growth? Why is their case acceptance running above 80%, while you can go all day without even presenting a new treatment plan?

You can only diagnose what you can see.

This seemingly obvious statement might be the most Zen statement in all of specialty medicine. At first glance, you may nod along. "Of course! I can't diagnose invisible things, or conditions that aren't there. I can only treat the people in front of me. To diagnose and treat more people, I obviously need to work harder and increase my patient load."

That misses the point. You see, when it comes to dentistry, I tend to be on the side of the CE junky. They're always looking to learn new skills, build connections with new specialties, and increase their understanding of oral-systemic health. As a result, if a new practitioner and the CE see the same patient, they see two totally different mouths. The CE junkies see a multitude of potential issues and options and use them to create a path to health for their patients. At the moment they diagnose a patient, they can also see what the end result of treatment, or lack of treatment, will be. They present more cases and have higher treatment acceptance than younger colleagues because they can take in more information and make more connections. They see more.

If you want to diagnose more and treat more, you need to start by seeing more. This goes for business opportunities too. Other, more successful practitioners aren't getting more opportunities than you do. They're just better at seeing opportunities around them. Where you see random events, they see business opportunities.

There's actually a psychological phenomenon that can help us learn to see the opportunities around us.

It's called the Baader-Meinhof phenomenon or, more generally, the frequency illusion. The idea is that when you focus your attention on something, you start seeing it everywhere. Not because you're imagining things, but because these things were always there—your brain was ignoring them before, in the interest of efficiency.

The problem is that sometimes the brain ignores information that's actually vital to peak function. You've probably seen the results of this reality editing in your own life. Have you ever tripped over a chair because someone moved it? Or tried to sit and started to fall, because the chair that had been there was no longer there? It's impossible to take in all of the constant stimuli in our environment, so our brain spends a lot of time filling in gaps. "Everything is the same as before. No need to look for the chair; the chair is always there." Boom! Suddenly you're flat on your back and your kids are laughing at you.

Baader-Meinhof is a way to get your brain to do the opposite trick—to start noticing things and to scan the environment for certain items.

For instance, "Have you noticed how many blue houses there are in this town?" Chances are you haven't, but now you will, and they'll be everywhere. Or, in a dental office, "Have you ever noticed how many patients need incisal-edge composites?" At the optometrist, "Have you ever noticed how many patients might really benefit from laser surgery?" At the chiropractor, "Look at all of our patients who'd do better with more frequent appointments." Boom...they're everywhere. Even after just reading this.

Use it on your patients. "Aren't you amazed how many people are looking for a good <insert your specialty here>?" They'll start noticing people who would love to be referred to your office, even if five minutes ago they couldn't think of a single referral.

Most of all, use this tactic on yourself, so that you stop missing those opportunities that the other guys are seeing. Ask yourself the following questions.

- How many local businesses might be interested in a contract relationship as a benefit for their employees?
- Where can I market my practice, where people will be predisposed to want the services I provide?
- Which of my employees are doing a really great job?
- Where am I wasting time and creating bottlenecks in my practice?
- What new services aren't readily available in my area but are needed?
- What traits do my best patients share?
- What continuing education courses really address my current business needs?
- When during the day do I have time to work on the business instead of working on patients?
- What barriers to treatment do my patients most commonly present?
- How many times a day do I get off topic and off track during case presentation?

Sit down with your team and brainstorm. Just stretching yourselves and trying to observe new things will open up new avenues and new opportunities to improve and grow. Remember, if you're not actively looking for new ideas, you'll always just see more of the same.

For an extra challenge, start a "Baader-Meinhof Question of the Day." Ask it at your morning team meeting, and have everyone get back together at the end of the day and list what they discovered. You'll find it's like turning your entire team into a supercomputer, focused on solving the problem of the day.

COURSE 9

Credit Worthy vs. Payment Worthy, and Your Business

The economic ups and downs of the last twenty years have left many of our patients in a strange situation. The economy is growing again, and unemployment rates are dropping. In some places, they're at less than 3%, and in April 2018, the national average was 3.9%. It doesn't matter what the federal minimum wage is. Look at what your local McDonald's or Walmart is paying new employees. People are going back to work, and they're finally ready to have those procedures and therapies they've needed for years.

This is great news for practitioners like us. People need us, and they can pay us. So why is this situation worth a whole chapter in my book? People have money again, but many of them don't yet have credit ratings or savings to match. Our country is coming off one of the worst financial crashes and recessions in history.

The Dallas Federal Reserve estimates that in the recession, US households lost between 50K and 120K each in assets and potential earnings. Then, on top of that initial loss, health problems, stress, and other issues related to the financial crash slowed recovery down to a crawl. We've been in a huge hole, and we're only just now crawling out of it.

Many of our patients have suffered huge financial setbacks due to job loss or health issues. Not all real estate has recovered from the crash, so for many people, tapping into equity is impossible. If they made it through the crisis by leaning on credit cards, they're probably maxed out paying down debt but unable to get any new loans.

So here's the problem. There are people who need work done, who have stable jobs, but who can't draw on savings or credit cards to pay up front. As a practitioner, what can you do for these people, when options like care credit are off the table? You have a few options:

- You can give them a treatment plan and encourage them to save up, knowing full well that their situation may get worse before they can save up the money for you.
- You can offer them a less expensive but less effective treatment that they can afford up front.
- You can "be the bank" for patients who will make regular payments but whose current credit ratings put more traditional financing options out of reach.

Of these four options, only the last will allow you to make more money, do more procedures, and transform more lives. Too many of us shy away from this option because it sounds scary. Are we going to have to carefully calculate interest and expenses? Will we have to get a special license? Are our office teams going to have to become collections agents?

The answer to most of these questions is "probably not". Yes, you'll have to do some math up front about the odds of getting paid, but you'll quickly find that, when you offer a way for someone to get work done with a monthly payment, they'll follow through. People are used to buying on time now—it's how they purchase their new phones. They get the phone up front, and then they're paying a monthly fee to cover it for the next year or two. It just makes sense to finance non-emergency procedures and therapies based on the monthly cost, not the total cost.

Offering this service to your patients also makes sense. A couple of hundred dollars a month spread out over 12 to 18 months seems more affordable than $4000 up front.

Charging Based on the Likelihood of Repayment

Banks would never loan money to people unless they had interest associated with it which offsets the inherent risk of lending. But, as a practice owner, I'll take a 10% discount on my fee so I can get my money upfront. That's typical for us. Changing how we manage fees and payments requires us to make a 180° shift in our thought process. This is a true paradigm shift that allows practitioners to create more revenue and help more patients than they've ever been able to help in their entire practice career.

Patients can make monthly payments with interest for care, just like they make monthly payments with interest for new phones, television, cars, and furniture. The key is to vary the charge based on their likelihood of repaying the full debt. I like to rank patients from A to E, with A being the best credit and E being the worst. Then I set interest rates as follows.

- Pays total upfront: No interest, obviously
- A credit score: 9.9%
- B credit score: 11.9%
- C credit score: 13.9%
- D credit score: 15.9%
- E credit score: 17.9%

Even someone with excellent credit and money in the bank may choose to finance their care, because cash is king today. No one wants to be left with an empty bank account, especially since health insurance deductibles are rising and they want to be prepared for emergencies. From that perspective, 9.9% interest isn't much. So, they hang on to their cash, and then what happens is they make monthly payments to you. With these people, the chances of them defaulting on a note is less than 1%.

Some doctors say, "Well, I'm ok getting notes out to the A, B, and C patients, but I'm nervous about the D and E patients." But I know many doctors who say, "I'm ok doing financing on any patient, A through E." Are they crazy?

Well, let's look at the statistics. We know that the Es are people with poor credit. 11.7% of them default on the notes. That means that more than 88% of the people are making their payments. And you're charging 17.9% interest. So, the interest from the 88% who do pay off their notes more than covers the loss from the patients who don't pay you.

Hints for Long-term Financing In-office

- Keep payments under $400 month, even if you have to stretch the timeline. A recent study found that 40% of American adults can't cover a $400 emergency expense immediately.

- For more expensive procedures and therapies, require the first two to three months in advance. This means that either the patients can wait two to three months to start treatment or make a larger down payment at the start of treatment.
- Third parties exist that will draw up the contracts and collect payments, so that you can be sure the arrangements are legal and so that patient questions don't tie up your already busy office staff.

In general, a doctor's tolerance for risk in financing grows as he sees how many of his patients pay him back with interest, and how monthly payments help him expand his practice rapidly on a stable foundation. The financing system allows him to do more high value procedures every day and sends the hourly productivity for the practice through the roof. And it's not just about making more money. Suddenly you're able to help patients who you would have had to send away. You got into this field because you enjoy restoring the sick to health. Changing how you finance means that you can spend your days focusing on your most high value and emotionally rewarding procedures. You can rediscover your joy and enthusiasm for your practice.

Chapter Sources

1 *https://www.dallasfed.org/~/media/documents/research/staff/staff1301.pdf*

2 *https://www.cnbc.com/2018/05/22/fed-survey-40-percent-of-adults-cant-cover-400-emergency-expense.html*

COURSE 10

Hedonic Adaptation and the Work-Life Balance

Everything is amazing. We live in the wealthiest country on Earth and can reasonably expect to live long, healthy lives. We work in exciting fields, help people every day, and earn enough to give our families the gift of financial security. We can learn new information and skills without ever leaving our offices, and if we don't like the weather somewhere, it's easy to travel for a change of scenery. It's a great time to be alive. So why do so few practitioners seem truly happy? Most successful people don't feel successful. Instead, they feel like they're always running at full speed but never catch up to the rest of the pack.

The psychological term for this is "hedonic adaptation". Simply put, it's the high-achiever's treadmill of doom. We set a goal, we achieve that goal. We get a bump in self-efficacy and self-worth and life is great...but only for a short while.

Inevitably, all success before a certain moment becomes moot, and we begin to pursue the next goal that's going to connect those dots and fill that hole and *this time* the feeling of success is going to last. Round and round we go, constantly chasing and achieving, buying and acquiring. If you're not growing, you're dying; and we've still so much we need to do.

Do you know any successful adults who aren't 99% exhausted?

Chuck Palahniuk, the novelist best known for *Fight Club*, said, "We buy things we don't need, with money we don't have, to impress people, we don't like." Far too many people fall into the spending trap. The thinking is obvious. If I can surround myself with the symbols of success, then I must be successful, and I will feel successful.

There's a bumper sticker that says, "Somewhere, someone with less than you is happy." Maybe, but as I've mentioned, I guess I'd rather be sad in a big house with a boat than happy in a shack. This might sound materialistic, but the simple truth is that many of us don't know how to do anything but keep striving for the next big thing. For some of us, this sense of being driven is a good thing. We're at a point in our life where it's ok for everything to take a back seat to our careers. However, others of us desperately need to learn how to be at peace with where we're at in the present. If we don't, we're going to have a lot of dark days, right up until our very last one.

Many successful practitioners fall into this trap because they don't realize that they're making sacrifices. Instead, they look back and see a long line of obvious decisions. These high achievers are nobody's victims, and they fail to see the impact of their choices on those around them, because to them, there was no other reasonable path to take. In most cases, they'll claim the long hours and neglect are somehow on behalf of those they love. By the time they realize that their focus on work came at the expense of their most important relationships, it's too late to rebuild. They may have succeeded in their careers, but they've failed at being human.

They've been motivated by the belief that each choice is leading them closer to that final goal: the finish line where they know they left it all on the table. They believe that when this day comes, they're going to sleep for a week. But this day never comes, and anything that resembles a finish line is quickly replaced with a new one...the real one.

Life is what happens while you're making other plans. Real life isn't big; it's very small. We feel compelled to push it to a larger, grandiose stage, but when you break it all down, the only things that really count are the people around you. If you don't believe me, pull out your phone or a picture album and see which pictures you enjoy the most. It's never cars, houses, or landscapes—it's always the pictures that captured a memory.

Over a trillion pictures are taken annually. The question to ask is, how many do people go back and look at? Very few. We're too busy searching for the next hit of endorphins from getting likes on some photo of our food to actually experience the time we have with the people around us. For high achievers who thrive on feelings of winning, social media is a drug whose highs and lows quickly replace the smaller dramas and rewards of interacting with the people in our lives. But the wins on social media are illusions, and the slow, hard work of building relationships with your spouse and children leads to greater rewards. It's the difference between someone who prepares for retirement by playing the lotto and someone who dutifully saves part of their paycheck in a dull IRA. Little sacrifices over a long time result in a happier life.

Older practitioners have often learned all of these lessons the hard way, but if you're still fooling yourself about what will make you happy, these rules can get you on track to a better future:

1 Phone off at six o'clock, unless you're coordinating social plans. Otherwise, no. If there's an emergency at the office, it's better to get a good night's sleep and find out about it in the morning anyway.

2 No phones until after breakfast. The screen should not be the first thing to get your attention in the morning. That respect belongs to your spouse or your children. They deserve it and so do you.

3 Phones in a stack when out to dinner; if someone checks their phone, they owe the table a round of drinks.

4 Everyone helps with dinner and everyone helps clean up. No divisions of labor and no phones. You'll be amazed how much better your day and your communication gets.

5 Never get one dog, always two, and walk them as a family unit. After dinner is the perfect time. It'll keep your energy up and the communication flowing.

6 Always go to bed at the same time as your significant other, phones off. This should be coveted time to discuss the day and plan for tomorrow. If your spouse stops being important, no problem; you can practice on your next one, and the next, until you get it. But it will be pretty expensive, and all of your hard work will be going to alimony and child support.

7 Flirt with your spouse in public. This goes for both sexes.

8 If you have work to do in the evening, don't. It's a trap. Go to bed at your normal time and get up early. Your mind will be sharp, and you'll complete the work much more easily.

9 Protect your vacation time. If your employer doesn't care that much about you, then why do you care so much about them? If you're the boss, then treat yourself with the same respect you'd give to your team. Your practice won't fall apart in your absence, and if it does, that's a valuable data point for how you need to reorganize.

10 Mentally compliment every single person you pass every single day. It'll boost your mood and teach you to look for the good in everyone. This includes the person in the mirror.

The main factor in work-life balance isn't your income, your career arc, or your ambitions. It's the small choices you make every day. Start making better choices, and the rest will fall into place.

COURSE 11

What Beer at a Baseball Game can Teach us About Pricing Procedures

As a species, we generally make poor choices when it comes to money. To really understand, we only need to look at a few examples.

When people feel uncomfortable and are dealing with unfamiliar subject matter, their defenses tend to skyrocket. They're terrified of being taken advantage of or looking foolish. Ask any mechanic, dentist, or lawyer and they'll all have a seemingly endless supply of customers' hilarious (and troubling) reactions to prices.

What makes this so confusing is the multitude of ways people willingly spend enormous sums of money with little to no expectation of known equivalent value. Take the price of a beer at a baseball game. If that same beer was to be purchased by the case for $15.00, that beer would cost you $0.60. In most stadiums, a not very good beer is going to run you at least $8.00. There may be a decent amount of griping, but for each person that passes, there's someone else buying two...or even more.

Imagine if this occurred in other areas of life. If the decent $20.00 ribeye steak you could grill at home was going to cost you $260.00 at a restaurant, two things would happen. First, we'd never go out to eat again and second, we'd all be opening up restaurants.

Now, clearly this shifting reaction to prices isn't magic. It's basic economics and simple psychology. Mentally, we're continually creating micro-budgets based on the things we need or want to do. Knowing that beer can be purchased for $0.60 later doesn't do you any good when you're at the ballpark.

Most attendees plan to buy a beer or soda and some food. They know this ahead of time; they plan for it. They pay the ridiculous amount and don't feel the least bit ashamed. Those add-ons are the price of the experience. We love the romantic notion of the American baseball experience and once we're in those seats, we're not going to let a little thing like money get in the way of a good time.

We see these patterns repeat in many areas of our life. Most people budget enough to make their car payments, but the second they need new tires they act like Goodyear and Illuminati are conspiring to rip them off. There's little to no consideration for the fact that those tires are arguably the item on the car most responsible for keeping you alive!

We budget for cars, but we don't budget for tires. We budget for vacations and new phones, but we certainly don't budget for medical emergencies. People enjoy spending money on fun experiences and luxuries. They hate spending money on unpleasant things. This causes people to feel better about the oddly expensive three hours of baseball rather than a necessary or life-changing procedure that will make them happier and healthier for years to come.

So, now you know. Patients are rejecting life-changing procedures because they're just not fun like overpriced pretzels and beer. To increase case acceptance and your overall acceptance, you have to address these objections head on.

Oddly, most offices still only address money questions once they're asked. If we wait until asked, we're forced to be reactive. Controlling the financial conversation keeps the office in control. Your expertise is a lot like those tires we talked about. Some patients are proactive and will have work done before there's a crisis. Others wait until they experience the equivalent of a blowout on a 100-mile stretch of deserted highway at midnight.

To start changing the conversation, add these elements to your case presentation.

1 Compare the cost of proactive treatment to the cost of a worst-case scenario treatment down the line. "If you let this go until you're in crisis, it will cost you $10,000 just to get back to where you are today. If we deal with it now, I can actually improve your situation for $5,000."

2 Start with the risks of not treating, then move to the benefits of prompt treatment—like better appearance, less pain, and improved function. Help your patients see that it's not, "You have to do this," but, "You want to do this."

3 Include testimonials and before-and-after pictures. People buy pricey beer at a ball game in part because everyone else is buying and enjoying the beer. Let your patients see

that other people are choosing this treatment...and loving the results.

4 Make financing available in manageable chunks. It's easier to stomach the overpriced food and drink at a ball game because you're paying in installments as you buy each item, not one big food fee as you enter the park. Tires hurt because they're expensive and you have to pay all at once. New phones don't hurt because the cost is spread out. So quote the cost in monthly payments, not a lump sum.

What you have to offer is better than the weak beer of a baseball game. Change how you share treatment plans with your patients and help them appreciate that fact.

COURSE 12

How Motivational Interviewing Will Increase Your Production

Before you read any further you should know one thing. I'm psychic. Don't believe me? Think about the last 10 or 20 new patients you saw. Now think about how those interactions went. I can see them in my mind. 75% of them looked like this:

1. You attempted to prove that the patient had a problem (if they did).
2. You educated the patient on the benefit of change or treatment.
3. You warned of them of the consequences if they didn't change.
4. You told the patient how to change so these things wouldn't happen.
5. You got really frustrated when they refused to change and you began to question your career choices.
6. Repeat.

Much of the issue boils down to the fact that people generally resist change, and many health problems have a behavioral component to them. Meanwhile, we're in our field because we're natural fixers. So we have a patient resistant to change, and a practitioner who wants to force change as quickly as possible. No wonder we butt heads and walk away in despair!

Imagine we ran a tire shop, and each and every morning many of our clients woke up and threw a fresh box of nails into their driveways. They'd then come in every six months complaining about the rough ride and the poor quality of tires you sold them. In reality, there's no point in fixing the tires until they're willing to pick up the nails.

Break the Addiction to Bad Habits

We need new tools. Desperately. Motivational Interviewing (MI) is one tool that can empower your patients to make good choices and ultimately give them better outcomes. The technique was originally developed to help people suffering from addictions overcome those addictions and re-enter normal society. However, it has applications when dealing with anyone whose choices are negatively affecting their health and relationships. While motivational interviewing is certainly no panacea, the techniques provide tools and methods that keep us from fighting the wrong fights and help us to recognize the signals given to us by patients who are truly ready to change.

One of the MI thought leaders, David Rosengren, gave us a simple acronym to remember: **DARN.** Desire, Ability, Reasons, and Need. All four of these factors must be in place for a patient to take an active role in their treatment. By using Motivational Interviewing, we can help patients recognize that they have all of these traits, and that they are ready to change and live a healthier life. If a patient doesn't have these underlying traits, MI can't help them accept and participate in a treatment plan. But if they have them, MI can make all the difference in outcomes.

No change happens without the **desire** to change. If someone is unhealthy but content, why should they change their lifestyle or opt for an uncomfortable procedure? There's no reason to choose discomfort and change when the status quo is good enough.

Ability is truly the most limiting of all the signs. It's no secret that if medical treatments were free, people would have more of them, especially the cosmetic kind. Budgets are real, and often impossible to alter for people on fixed incomes; but there are always behaviors and commitments that can be made without a financial cost. And if a patient has the ability to make the low or no-cost changes, then financing becomes a better option, because they've already adopted the new habits that will make the procedure generate great benefits. If you find a patient who's able to do the hard work of change, it might be worth it to give them care at cost further down the road. They'll be a raging success story, a great testimonial, and bring in more production than you gave up by waiving some of the fees.

Reasons. Change rarely happens in a vacuum. Ask questions until you've found the trigger for change. Often people have suffered for years or contemplated a given procedure for decades. Why are they here now? What happened to turn years of thinking into action? Often something simple can be just enough to get the ball in play: a hurtful truth from a child, an upcoming reunion, or a divorce. Why now? This question aligns the goals of the office and patients. We're a vehicle to that solution, not an obstacle.

Need. Finally, there needs to be a problem to fix. This is very closely tied to desire, but it's not entirely redundant. Doctors often fall into what MI practitioners refer to as the "righting reflex." If they see something broken, then the patient needs to get that fixed. Well, if we really get down to brass tacks, the patients don't *need* perfect health, function, or appearance; but we assume most would certainly prefer them. There are some patients who only *need* to be out of pain. If it doesn't hurt, then they'll wait. Sound familiar? Don't forget, I'm psychic.

If all of the DARN factors seem to be present, it's time to use MI practices to work together for a solution. If any are lacking, you can still present the case, but be ready for your patient not to be ready yet. It's not wasted time—things change, and you'll see this person again in a few months or a few years. But go into the presentation assuming that you're sowing the seed for future encounters, not effecting immediate change.

What is a Motivational Interview?

The basic framework of a Motivational Interview is the following.

- Express empathy while practicing reflective listening.
- Help patients work through the discrepancy between their treatment goals and current bad habits.
- Avoid argument and confrontation. You're their companion on a journey, not a dictator.
- Adjust to patient resistance rather than opposing it. If a patient is especially resistant on a certain point, move on. You're not trying to win. You're trying to help them clarify their own position so that they can commit to change.

- Encourage optimism and self-efficacy. Motivational interviewing involves being a bit of a cheerleader. You believe they can change. Help them believe they can change.

Reflective listening involves three main steps: asking an open-ended question, affirming their answer, and then summarizing what the patient has learned about themselves.

How to Ask an Open-Ended Question

A good rule of thumb for reflective listening is the 70/30 rule. The patient should be doing 70% of the talking. Asking open-ended questions invites the patients to share with us how motivated or willing to change they are.

Example:

"Why do you think your teeth broke down like this?"

"Why are you unhappy with your appearance?"

"What habits could you change to be healthier?"

"What would you need to change to make this procedure worth having?"

Most patients have thought about these questions. Let them share their thoughts. However, if they slip into negative self-talk and despair, stop the line of thought and redirect. We're trying to motivate, not depress.

How to Affirm an Answer

State back to the patient what they told you, but framed as the solution to the problem.

"So, Mrs. Jones, it sounds like if we got you fixed up and found a way to cut back on the soda, and if you wore that night-guard and stayed regular with your cleanings, we'd have a good chance of this lasting the rest of your life; did I understand that right?"

"Since your blood pressure is a big risk factor here, it sounds like controlling it with diet, exercise, and medication might help you get it to a level where we can do this procedure safely; is that correct?"

"You'll be able to handle recovery from the surgery as long as you line up childcare and help at home in advance, is that correct? And you're thinking of asking your mother to come stay for a few weeks? That would be fantastic!"

Self-efficacy is big part of change. The patient must truly believe that they're capable of the change. In this example, we've simply proven to the patients that they know exactly what do to, and that they've even come up with a plan to effect the change. They're not helpless. They're competent. They have the resources they need to make the change.

Now, the wisdom behind this method is that it's no longer the doctor's responsibility to tell the patient what they need to do. The patient self-educates and, in doing so, volunteers themselves to be the only person truly responsible for the outcome. When there's no one else to blame failure on, you become more motivated to succeed.

How to Summarize and Seal the Deal

To be clear, "seal the deal" simply refers to an agreed-upon course of action, not necessarily treatment. That being said, we're not here to save the manatees, we're here to save health, function, and appearance while running a successful practice, so we need to be effective agents of change and help the patient get started on the necessary work.

Never ask the patients where or how they'd like to start. Too many choices breeds indecision. Instead, give a clear choice. "Mrs. Jones it sounds like we know exactly what we need to do, and I truly believe you're going to keep up your end of the deal. Knowing that, I recommend we start with *X* or *Y*. However, considering your concerns and plans, you'd be happier with *X*."

If you're fee for service, take price out of the equation, using a technique called dominated alternatives. Take the total of the treatment plan and cut it up however you'd like, as long as it's all even.

In conversation, it sounds like this:

"Mrs. Jones, it sounds like we know exactly what we need to do, and I truly believe you're going keep up your end of the deal. Knowing that, I recommend we start with *X* or *Y*. Financially, it's all the same. However, considering [reasons from above], you'd be happier with *X*."

When you use Motivational Interviewing, you're suddenly not the dictator, coming down from on high with tough, expensive plans. Instead, you're a helper, someone who your patient is trusting to help them meet their goals on their timeline. MI allows you to take the adversarial element out of many doctor-patient relationships. Stop arguing, and get back to doing what you trained to do: helping and healing.

Chapter Sources

1 *https://www.ncbi.nlm.nih.gov/books/NBK64964/*

COURSE 13

How Micromanagement is Destroying Your Practice, Your Team, and Your Production... and What to Do About It

If you're reading this book, you're either a recovering micromanager, or you're about to become one. In general, everyone who buys a practice goes through a micromanagement phase. At the time, it seems like a good idea. You're the expert. You went to school for years to reach this moment. And your entire future, and the future of your family, is totally dependent on the success of your practice. You have loans. You have kids who constantly need new shoes or stitches or trips to baseball camp. You have a house. You have a spouse who doesn't want to live off of dried beans, rice, and ramen. *The practice must succeed, and everything is riding on you.*

Micromanagement is human nature, especially if you're the sort of human who could make it through college, medical school, residency, and your first job working for someone else. You know it all. You have a perfectionist streak. And failure has never been an option. Meanwhile, your team doesn't have your education or experience. They're on salary and can get other jobs, so they're not as invested in your success. Worst of all, they may be doing things *inefficiently*, or even *wrong*. Of course you have to keep an eye on them, direct them, and limit their agency. It's the only way to make things work, right? You can singlehandedly drag your practice to higher production and more patients, even if everyone else is constantly thwarting you like a toddler thwarts his parents' attempts to keep a clean house. And this will be best for everyone, right?

Wrong. It's a recipe for disaster. A friend told me about a man she knew who was a dedicated micromanager. In fact, he believed there was only one right way to make orange juice from one of those cans of concentrate and would loudly defend his method. This young man got married. His wife had a different way of making juice. The juice still got made, it still tasted the same, but her method was different, and, to his mind, less efficient. So, he did the natural thing. He stood behind her every time she made juice and told her what to do, how to do it, and what she was doing wrong. How long do you think that marriage lasted?

Your relationship with your team can be a little like a marriage. You're partners, working toward a common goal. You hope that you'll work well together and that you'll have a long, successful collaboration. Now, if you treat your team like the man in the anecdote treated his wife, what do you think will happen? It won't be success, productivity, and new patients. It will be a long, grim death march to failure.

When you micromanage, you:

1. **Become unlikeable.** You can tell yourself it's better to be feared than loved, but you're lying to yourself. When you micromanage, you carry tension and accusation everywhere you go. Your team is stressed. Patients pick up on that and see your office as a miserable place. You, in turn, soak in the negativity around you and start to hate your job.
2. **Demean your team.** Why did you hire your team members? Because you thought they'd be good at the job. When you micromanage, you tell them over and over again, "You are a worthless incompetent."
3. **Prevent growth.** How do people learn new things? By being given a task, trying, failing, and recalibrating. When you micromanage, you try to program your team like robots, which locks them into a set range of choices and actions. You deny them the chance to learn, grow, innovate, and improve. And when you cripple your team this way, you cripple your practice.
4. **Lose productivity.** When the young husband was standing over his wife criticizing her OJ-making skills, he was using time that could have been used for something else, *and the same amount of OJ got made.* Micromanaging doesn't increase your production. Instead, you're sitting there focused on some menial task that will get done anyway when you *could* be diagnosing more conditions, presenting more cases, and performing more procedures.
5. **Pass blame onto others for your own bad habits.** "Well, I have to micromanage, or else they'll screw up." "I'm the only one around here who knows how to do things right." If this is the state of your office, it's your fault, not your team's. Your

need to be in control and your inability to teach and train others is what's causing the issue, not your team's laziness or stupidity. Because if they were actually stupid and lazy, you wouldn't have hired them to begin with, right?

Breaking out of the Micromanagement Trap

So, is it possible to save a practice that has been micromanaged for years? *Yes!* I did it! The key is to prepare your team to take responsibility, to force yourself to step back, and to give someone the authority to tell you when you're overstepping bounds again. Here are some tactics that can help you make the shift:

- **Make a sincere apology.** You've been unfair to your team. So apologize for micromanaging and for not treating them like competent professionals. Admit you were wrong. Promise to try to do better, while acknowledging that it will be a tough habit to break.
- **Make a list of tasks, who can do them, and who enjoys them.** In every practice there are some tasks only the doctor can do, which varies by state and specialty; some tasks that require certain skills in math, computers, or interpersonal interactions; and some tasks that certain team members enjoy more than others. Figure out who is capable of which tasks, and who enjoys which tasks. Delegate accordingly. You don't have to delegate *all* the tasks outside your practice specialty. For instance, some doctors really enjoy handling their own marketing. It's like a game to them. Others really enjoy dealing with computers. If there's a low-production task that you actually enjoy, it's all right to keep doing it. Just be ready to reassess if it starts to be a drag on your practice, and don't try to do *everything*.
- **Communicate larger goals and vision.** For your team to be able to work independently of your supervision, they need

to know what the goals are. That way, you're all going in the same direction, even if the paths you take aren't identical.

- **Write down the most important procedures and checklists.** This puts your team in charge of following procedure, but also gives them the tools they need to make the transition.
- **When you see a consistent mistake, organize a whole-team training.** Everyone needs refreshers sometimes, and there's no shame in that.
- **For important mistakes, correct in private.** Micromanagement shames people. Good management helps them correct mistakes but doesn't ridicule them in front of their peers.
- **Praise improvements, successes, and useful innovations in public.** To help your team recover from micromanagement, build them up. Praise them. Thank them. Give them an emotional stake in the success of your practice.

You won't be able to change your management style all at once. You'll backslide some. There will be bad days. Team members may make mistakes. Hang in there and keep improving. You're laying the groundwork for explosive growth down the line, because you're letting your team truly be a team, not a group of browbeaten servants.

COURSE 14

How PeeWee Basketball Can Transform Your Business

The last time I was at a Peewee basketball game, I saw a great example of business instincts in action. And the funny thing is, those seven-year-old kids had a better grasp of business principles than many people in our field do.

There are two contrasting mechanisms that drive human nature. We're risk-seeking when dealing with unlikely gains, and we're risk-averse when it comes to protecting ourselves from loss.

A good basketball team, like a good business, can play both offense and defense and usually wins the day based on hard work and an ability to hustle. At my son's game, when a child scored a point, there was an 84% chance that the same child would be the first person down the court to play defense. In our game, this ratio was 21:25. If the scorer wasn't first, then he was the second, 100% of the time. Every kid on both teams, from the stars to the klutzes, exhibited the same behavior. It was like second nature to them.

There was no role-based rationale for this. These kids aren't old enough to play position well. Instead, their games are chaos. Outside of this one fact, you couldn't guess where any given kid would be at any time. At this age, you'd think the scoring kid would get distracted while celebrating his basket and be the last down the court as he struggled to shift from victory back to the game in front of him. Yet, again and again, those kids switched quickly from offense to defense.

We all have the same, deep-seated instinct to protect our direct contributions and the resources we provide. In business, we often fail to see what is so clear to the PeeWee players. We prioritize the wrong metrics or put up barriers to communication that leave our "points" unprotected. We focus so much on scoring the next basket that we lose sight of how we're falling behind in the game.

To improve your business, look at how you protect what you've already achieved.

When you score a point in the office, are you the first one back on defense?

What would good defense even look like in your practice?

What good are top-line revenues when deals with PPOs, out of control attrition, and failing patient relations aren't protecting your efforts? Some owners play defense by agonizing over supply costs, raises, the thermostat setting, lights being left on, and a million other distractions that, combined, will barely move the bottom line. The fastest way for me to gain true insight into the state of a practice is to simply check the quality of the toilet paper they provide for employees. Bad toilet paper means a struggling business. The owner's defensive instinct is correct, but his defensive strategy is faulty and actually leads to more losses—no employee is going to stick around in a place where the owner is too cheap and frightened to spend the extra buck on decent toilet paper.

So, what should you look at instead? Energy efficiency may make you a friend to the local utilities, but it won't increase production. Instead, spend some time looking at your patient retention budget. Money spent attracting new patients is wasted if your old patients are walking out the door or those new patients don't stick around long enough to become regulars.

The kids on the Peewee team understand what many practice owners don't. It's a better long-term strategy to protect the points—patients—you already have than to ignore defense and count on shooting more baskets. On average, retaining a patient costs 1/5 as much as attracting a new one. In addition, if you take PPO plans, you need to see the patient a minimum of two, often three, times to even see a profit; so if you're not retaining PPO patients, your marketing is actually losing you money.

Defensive Plays for Your Practice

Develop defensive strategies that help you turn new patients into long-term ones. Basketball teams create and practice plays to navigate sticky situations. You need to create and practice your own plays to defend your new patient gains.

For example, here's an example of a solid defense against the patients who say they need to talk to their spouse about finances, when in reality they're just going to price-shop the treatment plan.

"Mrs. Jones, I'm glad you're going to talk to Mr. Jones. Treatment plans can be tough for patients to evaluate. Think about cars. When you need a new car, you know exactly what to do, where to look, and what questions to ask. Driving down the road, you can easily spot cars that won't be on the road in a few years, and some that shouldn't be on the road now. I want your car—your health—to be on the road for the rest of your life. If you're going to call around to a few other "dealerships" (pause for laughter), I can guarantee you that we'll never be the least expensive. But I can also tell you that after folks do make those calls, the vast majority choose to put their faith in us. Just in case that's true for you too, I suggest we go ahead and make the appointment, but we'll put it in pencil. In a few days, if we don't hear anything, we'll switch it to pen. Does that sound fair?"

There's no pressure in this defense. It adds no additional work for anyone, and most of the time, the penciled-in appointment ends up written in pen.

Where do you need to improve your defense? To find out, start collecting data.

- How many patients leave your practice or go inactive every month?
- What are their reasons for leaving?
- How can you keep them active?
- What programs do you have to encourage patient loyalty?
- How do you address concerns and complaints and make them right?
- How do you let patients know you value them?
- Where are you too focused on new points, while letting events chip away at your lead?

Spend some time evaluating your team and the game you play. Be first on defense and you'll be in the championship game in no time.

COURSE 15

What Friedman and Handy Teach About Compensation, ROI, and the Point of Your Practice

Let's talk about corporate responsibility for a moment. What responsibilities do you, as a practice owner, have towards your community, your employees, and yourself? There's been a lot of argument about this over the last couple of centuries. Should you focus only on profit, and let employees and society take care of themselves? Do you put social responsibility first, and hope profitability follows? Is there some sort of happy medium or a magic ratio of profit versus social responsibility? In the last century, the two sides of the argument were articulated by economists Milton Friedman and Charles Handy.

Friedman had a very simple formulation to describe a business's responsibility:

"In [a free economy] there is one and only one social responsibility of business—to use its resources and engage in activities designed to increase its profits *so long as it stays within the rules of the game.*"

In Friedman's formulation, businesses ought to focus on following the rules and making money. If a society decides that business should also say, prioritize the environment or pay a certain minimum wage, then the legislature can enact rules to that effect and the business should follow those rules.

Handy's view is that capitalism, and the pursuit of profit, has created a failed society, that modern shareholders are little better than gold diggers or pirates, and that companies should abandon the concept of profit and instead start viewing themselves as "Wealth Creating Communities" with social missions instead of profit motives. In short, "Don't Be Evil," and be Google, not Walmart.

I'm inclined to agree with Freidman. In addition to running a successful practice, I also work as a small business consultant. Every day, I work specifically with practice owners who struggle to find a balance between earning money and changing the world.

In our industry, the average doctor is close to one million dollars in debt or lost opportunity cost before they've even seen their first patient. The stress is compounded by the fact that most of these new owners have never run so much as a lemonade stand, let alone a complex medical facility.

The teams are certainly privy to the production numbers. They see the dollars that they help produce coming in, but they're never exposed to the path every single dollar that comes into the practice takes.

Each dollar is rapidly gobbled up, by not only traditional business costs, but by the servicing of an incredible debt load. The doctors are certainly not compelled to disclose any financial information to the employees, but this creates an inaccurate sense that the doctor is pocketing the lion's share of the incoming payments while most of the team earns an hourly wage.

It's very easy to get a loan for a practice. The actuaries will tell you that they rarely foreclose, but an insider can tell you that most start-ups don't make it. They're sold or acquired by larger corporations or hospital chains. The bank doesn't care; they got paid.

It's incredibly common for me to discover in an office that the techs are making more than the owner. Owners make up endless excuses for why this has happened, and the fear that surrounds correcting the compensation. When I meet resistant docs, I just tell them to ask the team members to either co-sign on the loan or become a partner in the business. Obviously, they never want to do this. My point is simply that those who won't share in the risk don't deserve a disproportionate reward.

All the systems from the top line to the bottom line should be designed to be owner-centric. Friedman was correct here. If there is no profit, there is no business, and the team loses their jobs. If the owner is struggling, the practice isn't long for this world. The "wealth creation community" is the *result* of maximizing profit, not the main goal of the business.

Now, this doesn't leave Handy out in the cold. In our industry, we're often dealing with various compounds that are potentially very damaging to the health of the environment, the surrounding community, or our teams. Clearly, adhering to OSHA and all the various protocols for the disposal of these elements is costly and time-consuming, but our business interests don't trump the rights of others. Our physical ability to toss our waste in the river doesn't get us off the hook for any damage done down the river. On the other hand, as Friedman pointed out, the law already takes care of this problem. We don't need to be more environmentally conscious than legally required.

What about community responsibility? Should we sponsor Little League Teams, work for charity, or join the local "Quality of Life" organization? These are all good things. In many cases, these are actually helpful for profit; in our business, being an engaged, well-liked community member is often great marketing. But they can't be our *goal.* If you're so busy doing charity work that you can't service your debt and your business is failing, then you shouldn't be owning a practice. You should be a missionary somewhere.

If your goal is a successful, profitable practice, these other things, these extras, will follow from the profit. So, maximize productivity. Pay off your debt. Compensate yourself for your work. The profit, and the breathing room it gives you, is what lets you treat employees well, engage with the community, and serve others. Without the profit, you can't even stay afloat, and everyone ends up out in the cold.

Chapter Sources

1 Christensen, C. M., & Raynor, M. E. (2003). Why hard-nosed executives should care about management theory. *Harvard business review, 81*(9), 66-74. [Reading for Module 1 Live Sessions]

2 Handy, C. (2002). What's a business for? *Harvard Business Review, 80*(12), 49-56

3 Friedman, M. (1970, September 13). The social responsibility of business is to increase its profits. *The New York Times Magazine*

4 Christensen, C. M., & Van Bever, D. (2014). The capitalist's dilemma. *Harvard Business Review, 92*(6), 60-68

COURSE 16

Budgeting for Customer Experience 101

In the last couple of years, customer experience has been everywhere. It seems like there are consultants lined up outside every small businessman's door, trying to lecture us on how we can be more like Zappos, or Amazon, or even Disney. So, does this mean that the future of owning a practice involves installing animatronic singing pirates in your lobby, or maybe replacing the couches and chairs with flying elephants? Are you doomed if your practice is just a normal practice with normal furniture and normal décor?

Of course not. We're providing treatments, not family vacations. But that doesn't mean that customer experience is unimportant. And the sooner you give some thought to how your patients, their families, and even your team members experience the day-to-day life of your practice, the sooner your can increase production and create a more enjoyable working environment for yourself while you do it.

So, why does customer experience (CX) matter if we're not in the business of entertainment? Shouldn't our patients care about how competent we are, how many certifications we have, and what our infection or complication rate is? Why should we focus on CX instead of on perfecting our procedures?

Well, in the first place, things like post-surgical infections *are* a part of CX. If you have a lot of them, then your CX is very, very bad, and of course you need to focus on not making your patients sicker than they were when they first came to your office.

Here's the thing. You don't have a high infection rate, right? You are a skilled clinician. You take excellent care of your patients. Great! Most of your competitors are *also* skilled clinicians who take good care of patients. If they weren't, their malpractice insurance would have dropped them by now and they'd be working as a sales rep for a pharmaceutical company or something.

Yes, you might be marginally better at some procedures than some of the other guys, but not dramatically enough that your patients will be able to judge your practice based on clinical excellence. Clinical excellence is important, but it's not what attracts and retains patients, or convinces them to refer their family and friends.

What else can your practice compete on? Maybe price? Consumers can definitely understand and compare prices. But when you focus on price, you get involved in a fast race to the bottom, and pretty soon you can't service your debt or meet your other obligations, and you're back to eating ramen and tending bar like you did as an undergrad.

Focusing on CX frees you from competition based on price.

When you create a plan and budget for CX, you set yourself apart from other practices. It can be something simple. Nicer swag bags. Birthday cards. It can be technological: a mobile-friendly preregistration form. Responsiveness to patient text messages. Great in-office Wi-Fi so that patients can game or work while they wait for you. It can be related to patient movement through the office. Clear signage for restrooms. Short waits. Comfortable chairs in the exam rooms. The key is to create an experience that makes your patients unlikely to shop around based on price. Does it work?

Look at the restaurant business. Why can Red Robin charge more than McDonald's, even as McDonald's improves its burgers? Because Red Robin provides an experience that convinces people it's worth the extra money, even though in terms of dollars per nutritional value, McDonald's is a better buy. If it was a question of eating as efficiently as possible, McDonald's would win every time.

Or take motels. Is a Holiday Inn Express really worth twice as much as Super 8? Not if you're just looking for a safe place to crash for the night. But the experience at HIE is better, so people pay more for it. It's not competing on price, it's competing on experience.

Things like decoration, staff uniforms, even the sort of music you play all contribute to customer experience. Certain kinds of experiences attract certain kinds of patients. For instance, many specialists in cosmetic procedures aim for a spa-like vibe, so that their patients feel ready to be pampered with elective treatments. Meanwhile, specialists seeking to attract children will focus on cartoons, video games, entertaining murals, and great toys as prizes. That experience is great for attracting kids but won't attract cosmetic patients. Practitioners who cater to a broad patient base often have different waiting or exam rooms aimed at providing different CX to each cohort. CX matters, and it helps create the sort of patients who keep coming back and are devoted to your practice. And that, in turn, leads to a happy team and a happy you, since everyone would rather spend their days treating patients who are glad to be there.

So, how do you set a CX budget for your practice? Here are my recommendations for practices with various revenue levels.

Target: 100K a Month in Revenue

External Marketing: Keep levels where they are.

Internal Marketing: Hire a CX consultant to help you and your team improve CX.

- Have your team complete a total of 100 CE units in CX over the next 12 months.

Target: 200K a Month in Revenue

External Marketing: Increase by 20%.

Internal Marketing: Continue to work with CX consultant. Develop systems and processes to improve CX and increase referrals.

- Hire an intern to develop better online outreach.
- Have your team complete a total of 150 CE units in CX over the next 12 months.

Target: 300K a Month in Revenue

External Marketing: Continue at same level as before.

Internal Marketing: Work on your own leadership skills and on developing other leaders in your company.

- Hire an experienced advisor to help you develop your leadership skills and begin duplicating other leaders in your company.
- Hire a second intern to develop while the first one has already increased responsibilities.
- Have your team complete a total of 200 CE units in CX and leadership over the next 12 months.

Target: 400K a Month in Revenue

External Marketing: Continue at same level as before.

Internal Marketing: Continue with leadership training.

- Hire an experienced advisor to help you develop your corporate strategy for further business development and for your long-term exit plan.
- You may consider expanding your operation in the same location or have a second location.
- Have your team complete a total of 300 CE units in CX and leadership over the next 12 months.

Focusing on CX allows you to quickly level up your practice. And once you've achieved excellent CX, you'll have the resources necessary to focus on developing your business and securing your future.

COURSE 17

Anatomy of a Persuasive Radio Ad

Let's take a few minutes to talk about radio. Is radio advertising still worth it? According to a study from the Center for American Progress, 90% of Americans ages 12 and older listen to the radio at least once a week. In the car, at the office, even on hold, traditional radio is still a popular way to discover new artists, hear old favorites, and pass the time. More Americans listen to the radio than use social media or read the newspaper.

In many markets, radio advertisements are an affordable way to attract new patients, especially if you're a fee-for-service practice and offering elective or cosmetic procedures. Many stations will even handle recording the ad for you once it's written. But how do you write a persuasive radio ad?

Here's an example of a strong radio advertisement:

> Same Day Smiles: 30 secs
>
> Doctor:
>
> *We call it Same Day Smiles because that's the best way to describe it. You take a little snooze and you wake up with your*

> *dream smile. When I heard about this technique, I desperately wanted to perfect it. Most people who choose it aren't trying to be fancy or movie stars; it's not even about smiling in pictures. It's usually just about smiling in the mirror. It's pretty powerful when they realize that this beautiful smile now belongs to them. Each smile reminds me how much I love what I do, and I'm so proud to have brought the technique to Iowa.*
>
> Announcer:
>
> *Veranda Dentistry. Visit PULSEDENTIST.COM or call 515-421-8154 today to learn more about this special offer!*

Why does this ad succeed? It gets right to the point. It starts by relieving fear concerning procedures and proceeds to an aspirational note. Who doesn't want to see a beautiful smile when they look in the mirror? Finally, it finishes with the provider making a personal connection with the audience. He loves what he does, and he wants to help the listeners. While most people who hear this ad won't pull over and call right away, they'll look up the site later, if they want a better smile.

Now, here's an example of a weak advertisement:

> *You're obviously an early riser; not that you necessarily want to be, but because you need to get things done. Hi, I'm Chad Johnson, dentist and founder of Veranda Dentistry. I'm likely finishing my workout and getting to work by 6 AM for our executive appointments. Executive appointments at 6 AM allow for you to get to work without breaking up your day, and without missing a beat. Maybe you're even finishing third shift. Maybe you're a teacher who doesn't want to use PTO for a dental visit. We perform Invisalign, smile replacement, smile enhancement, 3D guided dental implants for tooth replacement, laser dentistry, same-day smiles, same-day crowns, and licensed massage therapy.*

Visit OldiesDentist.com, or call 555-555-5555, to schedule your 6 AM executive appointment with our hygienist and myself, Chad Johnson, at Veranda Dentistry.

The ad starts with unpleasantness: getting up early because you have to knock out unpleasant chores. It moves to discuss the executive dental appointments. Great. Another unpleasant chore. Ugh. It's six in the morning. I've barely finished my coffee, and you want me to think about the dentist? *No thanks*, Dr. Johnson. This ad induces *ugh* rather than enthusiasm.

Here's the same ad after it's been edited to provide a better emotional punch:

I love mornings. It always feels like the world slows down a bit, just for me. No traffic, no lines; everything is a little easier. In my life, lunch time is for lunch and my evenings are for my family.

I'm Chad Johnson, dentist and founder of Veranda Dentistry. I created my Sunrise appointments because I totally get it. Coming to Veranda Dentistry should never be a hassle. Let the bank handle that one. I think the lobbies are now open on odd number days, but only on a full moon, during a leap year? It's crazy.

At Veranda Dentistry, we perform Invisalign, smile replacement, smile enhancement, 3D guided dental implants for tooth replacement, laser dentistry, same-day smiles, and same-day crowns.

Veranda Dentistry, where you can literally wake up to new smile.

Visit OldiesDentist.com, or call 555-555-5555, to schedule your 6 AM appointment with our hygienist and myself, Chad Johnson, at Veranda Dentistry.

Suddenly, mornings have a positive association. Warm sunlight. Fresh starts. And so, by starting on a warm note, the advertisement leads the listener to warm thoughts about convenient, early dentistry.

Here's another example of an ad that starts out too negatively, so that the listener tunes out:

Background: soft upbeat acoustic country music

Older 60+ Male:

I have worked hard all my life and am about to retire. I wish I would have taken better care of my teeth along the way—I'm aware that my mouth needs a lot of work, but I'm confused as to what my real options are. (Sigh) I'm not sure dentures are for me.

Announcer:

Are you curious about other options?

Dr. Peter L. Thompson in Portales offers a new *technology called HYBRIDGE. Using cutting-edge digital techniques and 3D scanning, he can create durable, beautiful teeth that look and feel like your natural teeth.*

You don't have to be ashamed of missing teeth anymore. Dr. Thompson and his team have been helping people just like you all over New Mexico and West Texas enjoy beautiful and healthy smiles.

Before you just settle for dentures, you owe it to yourself to call Dr. Thompson and ask about HYBRIDGE.

Call 555-555-5555; that's 555-555-5555 or visit ThompsonSmiles.com.

And here it is, rewritten to be positive and engender enthusiasm instead of exhaustion and despair:

Background: soft upbeat acoustic country music

Older 60+ Male:

It's hard to explain. My driver's license says I'm 60, my mind tells me I'm 20, my body feels like I'm 40, but my mouth looks like I'm 90. I'm not doing dentures, no sir. I don't care how far I need to go, I need someone to fix this up how I want, the way I want.

Announcer:

Did you know the average patient drives over 50 miles to visit with Dr. Peter L. Thompson in Portales to solve this problem? His solution is known as HYBRIDGE digital techniques; with 3D scanning, he creates durable, beautiful teeth that look and feel like your natural teeth.

You've busted your butt your entire life. It's your turn now.

If dentures aren't for you, call Dr. Thompson and ask about HYBRIDGE. You'll be amazed what's possible.

Call 555-555-5555; that's 555-555-5555
or visit ThompsonSmiles.com.

Look at that strong finish. "If dentures aren't for you..." What active retiree wants to embrace dentures? This advertisement leaves the listener excited and hopeful about the options available.

So, how can you apply these templates to your own radio scripts?

1 Radio relies on sound and emotion. For a radio ad, the emotional impact is more important than nitty gritty details.

Leave the listener with a feeling of "I want to meet this doctor, he can help me."

2 Use different templates for different stations. Research user demographics first and tailor your ad to the audience.

3 Be to the point. Thirty seconds doesn't lend itself to rambling.

4 Testimonials can be powerful tools in the radio environment.

5 Be willing to take advice from the experts. Don't fall in love with your words; expect to have to cut ruthlessly.

6 Use tracking numbers so you can tell which ads attract customers.

7 Don't use special offers as your call to action. Competing on price and discounts is a loser's game. Market the fact that you have solutions to the listeners' problems, and that you're ready to help.

8 Keep it positive. People don't listen to the radio to be brought low; they listen to relax or get pumped up.

Especially in small to mid-sized markets, radio can be a powerful marketing tool. Give it a try, and reach people where they're at.

COURSE 18

The Truth about Bossholes[1]

Microsoft is one of the most successful companies on the planet. If you work or go to school, you probably use at least one Microsoft product. Bill Gates is a legend among entrepreneurs, and the company is ubiquitous enough to inspire both fanatical love and fanatical hate. We should all be like Microsoft, right? Not quite. It depends on which iteration of Microsoft you try to emulate. Five years ago, the company was in deep trouble. Not because of markets, products, or consumers, but because of bad management and bad organizational restructuring.

Microsoft organizes its employees into teams. Leadership evaluated each team using a method called *stack ranking*. This tournament-style method of employee evaluation was a favorite of Jack Welch, the former CEO of GE, famous for his utter disregard of employee happiness.

Stack ranking is simple. You rank your employees based on a variety of factors to create a bell curve. There are a couple of

1 *I gotta thank Dr. Mark Costas for that perfect term…you nailed it!*

people at the top, a couple people at the bottom, and most of the people somewhere in the middle. If you're trying to make lay-offs, you cut the bottom employees. If you're not, you issue them a warning, pointing out that they're at the bottom. Since the ranking is done within departments, every team has winners and losers, even the successful teams.

The ratings set employees against each other. Instead of teams working together to defeat the company's competitors, they became gladiators, locked in a death match, desperate not to be on the bottom or to take risks that might knock them down a peg. Steve Ballmer, the CEO at the time, boasted a 51% approval rating. Obviously, we know which side of the bell curve was voting for him.

It wasn't just the rating system. Under Ballmer, even the mission statement betrayed a loss of direction and a lack of focus. The original mission statement for the company was, "A computer on every desk and in every home, running Microsoft software." Short, to the point, and goal focused. Under Ballmer, it had become "Creating a family of devices and services for individuals and businesses that empower people around the globe, at home, at work and on the go for the activities they value most." Too wordy and no meaningful goals. What does it mean to empower people? Which devices and services? The new statement could work as well for Toys R Us as for Microsoft, and we know where Toys R Us ended up.

The market sensed the problem. The company had been trading flat for eight years and it was no secret they needed a change. At that time, Microsoft (MSFT) was trading for roughly $26.00 dollars a share. For a tech stock, that was incredibly low. Everyone assumed the age of Microsoft was over and that it had begun its long, slow descent into total irrelevance.

So, what did they do? And how can you use their experience to transform your own practice?

The first thing Microsoft did was commit to doing whatever it took to turn things around. They moved from divisional design to an organizational design. A divisional design treats each team as its own little company. An individual team's successes and failures affect that team and its budget. If Xbox is doing well, then it's not their problem that Internet Explorer is losing market share. Not their circus and not their monkeys.

In an organizational design, the company rises and falls as a whole. It's more organic. In your own life, if your liver fails, your brain doesn't say, "Well, I'm a success, so who cares?" If the heart fails, the stomach doesn't get to go merrily on its way. Organizational design unites everyone around the health of the whole body. It's no longer every team for themselves. Moving to organizational design also included a move away from stack ranking. No more "every man for himself." No more *Hunger Games*-style evaluations. Instead, everyone was working together, focused on a single goal.

The changes turned the company around. Today, in 2018, Microsoft is trading for $90.00.

Microsoft nearly lost everything Bill Gates had built because they adopted bad systems on the whims of bad bosses. At one point, the divisional design and the stack rating probably looked like great ideas, especially to those at the top of the stack. Maybe they were more efficient, or seemed simpler. But the people who put them in place didn't think carefully about incentives or how making life easier for HR would affect the business as a whole.

What steps do you need to take to ensure you're not creating systems, in the name of efficiency or otherwise, that will cause more problems than they solve? Ask yourself these four questions as you plan for the future of the practice.

- **What is our mission statement, purpose, or vision?** While this might sound hokey, people follow leaders. To lead, you must know where you're going, or at least where you'd like to go. Does your team know your 3-, 5-, and 10-year goals? Do you know your 3-, 5-, and 10-year goals? Maybe start with a next-week goal and build up. I'm not even kidding.
- **How am I developing my team?** Any team needs to make a simple commitment: "We agree to better this year than we were last year." What have you done to make sure every single person on the team can say, "I have improved?" CE is great, but personal development can be better. You don't hire roles, you hire people.
- **Are we trying new things?** If being uncomfortable is the worst thing that can happen, you need to push the envelope. Track and measure new scripts and tactics. Commit to everyone just thinking about crazy ideas for 30 minutes rather than another useless staff meeting. You're surrounded by minds...use them!
- **Do I and my team act like we're all in it together?** Does your front office gripe about your back office, or vice versa? Do your techs and assistants engage in constant jockeying for influence and position? Then the incentives you're creating need to change to promote a unified vision and teamwork. Patients don't want drama and conflict. They want to feel like they're coming into a family atmosphere, with everyone focused on their care. Stamp out the pettiness, and reward team spirit.

At the end of the day, what saved Microsoft wasn't a new invention or innovation. Does anyone even remember the Zune? It was proper leadership combined with a more focused mission and fully engaged workforce. These are strategies that will benefit any business, from the local bagel shop to your practice.

COURSE 19

Social Media Quote Success, or Real Success?

Remember when quotes were cool? Having a great quote in your back pocket was like having an intellectual pick-up line. You'd wait for the perfect moment to drop that little gem and just sit back to bask in the warmth of being an eight-second Aristotle. Next stop: Cold fusion, maybe perpetual motion, not sure, the weekend's pretty busy.

Thanks to social media, quotes have become noise and oddly contrary. Specifically, there seems to be a negative or inverse correlation between the number of success-oriented quotes on social media and the posters' actual success.

People like quotes because they give insight and meaning in short, small bursts. You don't have to dig in. You can nod along and move on. Occasionally quotes come with great power (and great responsibility). A memorized quote can light a dark time, help you make the right decision under stress, or ease tension and promote laughter (in the case of Yogi Berra). On a basic level, we all need those things. It's a quick pattern interruption that helps us realign our thoughts and double-down on our commitments—a stand-by mechanism, easily deployable, to wax that poetic notion that others have been here before and we too shall prevail.

The internet has diluted that power, both by bombarding us with good quotes pasted on saccharine backdrops and by confusing us with false quotes that totally miss the point of famous authors.

Enter the *mantra*. Now, don't get hung up on the word and any previous definitions you started reading with; we're defining our "mantras" as any simple, memorable phrase designed to motivate, encourage, or simply remind ourselves of what we're capable of.

I'm going to share one of my favorites with you. Because while you'll face many things that simply must be endured, like a bout of the flu, it's possible to train for most of the challenges, setbacks, and failures that you're bound to experience in your personal and professional life.

If you've ever sailed, rowed, swam or played near a body of cold water, you probably learned the 50-50-50 rule. This means that in 50-degree water, you have a 50% chance of making it 50 yards. In all the research that's been done, the people that survive in harsh conditions like that are simply the people that thought they would. So, while self-esteem—how you feel about yourself—is certainly important, self-efficacy—your belief in your ability to complete a task—is what's going to make it or break it when you hit inevitable bumps in the road. And just so you know, there are going to be some very big bumps in your personal and professional life. They're unavoidable.

So, the mantra you need to keep in your back pocket is:

Success is what success does

This Zen-ish phrase sets the tempo and perspective for all that you do. However, anything can be used for evil, and this phrase has been used as an excuse for excessive spending. Are the things you buy truly an accurate measure of success? We all know better than to say it is. There are a lot of sad people in very big houses.

In reality, success begins with self-actualization. We need to feed our talents and take steps to make the lives of those around us better. There are countless times in a day when you can ask, "What does 'success' do here? Does 'success' go to the gym or stay in bed? Does 'success' spend quality time with his/her family or watch a football game? Does 'success' seek opportunities that have impact or does 'success' wait to be invited to the dance? Does 'success' make sure that every important person in my life knows how important they are right now, or rather wait until a tomorrow that may never come?"

It's not about money; it's about behavior, action, and control. Powerless is not an option. One of the best applications of this mantra is *Success doesn't make sacrifices, success makes choices.* You are not a victim. Don't like your job? Get a new one. Feel empty? Give back.

It even works for budgeting. A lot of young docs are a little giddy about finally earning a salary. It's time for the fancy new car, the professionally decorated house, the lavish vacations and memberships. When you feel tempted, remember *The Millionaire Next Door*. It turns out success lives within a budget and plans ahead to save for big indulgences.

So, what does success do?

- Success plans for the future.
- Success makes time for relationships.
- Success has goals and plans for attaining those goals.
- Success sees failure as an opportunity to recalibrate.
- Success is always learning and perfecting new skills.
- Success is kind to those without power.
- Success is prudent with resources, but not stingy or fearful.
- Success knows that the pie is not fixed and that the game is not zero sum.
- Success doesn't waste time on envy.
- Success is willing to innovate.
- Success seeks personal and professional growth.
- Success helps better the community.

The one thing we can all agree on is that none of us are getting out of this life alive. Bad things are going to happen. Get up and drown those experiences in good ones. Leave flowers on the door of a stranger; pay for the coffee of the person behind you. Give genuine compliments often and freely. Commit to this change and watch your life improve. And one more thing:

"Make your bed."

—Mom

COURSE 20

How the Nintendo Vacuum Can Teach You to Fail Well

History has no shortage of business and great ideas that just didn't make it. Just picture a support group with the leaders of Kodak, Blockbuster, Toy R Us, and Circuit City all sitting around going, "What happened??" For the record, they wouldn't let Sharper Image or Sky Mall into the group...anyone should have seen those failures coming a mile away.

The internet has created a hyper-competitive environment that most fee-for-service medical offices weren't prepared for. Suddenly, marketing and sales mattered more than clinical skill. Many offices failed to adapt, feeling insulated and protected by their longstanding presence in the community. Many amazing clinicians simply retired early or sold the practice rather than learning to adapt to the new marketplace. This exit was available to the first affected generation, but with the advent of social media, the rest of us have to live with a world where marketing is king.

For our practices to succeed, we need to be constantly adapting and changing. What works now will not always work. Heraclitus, the ancient Greek philosopher, reminds us that we "cannot step into the same river twice." Change is constant. Fish move. Water moves. Rocks and pebbles are eroded. The river changes. When there's a human element, like in business, change happens even more rapidly. The information you're processing now from the data you gathered last week may already be past its expiration date.

Nintendo, home of Mario and Link and Pokemon Go, is a great example of how a business can face change and failure yet still end up successful.

The Prologue

Founded in 1889 by Fusajire Yamauchi, Nintendo Koppai has always been primarily, though not exclusively, in the entertainment and leisure business. The original popularity of the company was based on a set of playing cards. These handmade cards were used for a variety of games and the Kyoto-based company quickly grew.

The business model was unchanged until the 1950's, when they began to print the cards on plastic. This meant lower-cost production and a more durable product. Around this time, the grandson of the founder realized that their business model was too limited. For the company to grow, they must innovate.

The Crisis

In 1959, they struck proverbial gold by signing a licensing agreement with Disney. With the popular characters on the cards, the product exploded in popularity. Nintendo went public only three years later.

Sometimes failure comes fast on the heels of success. The sudden influx of cash almost killed the company. Nintendo ambitiously drifted away from their core competencies and began chasing dollars through other business entities. They launched everything from a taxi company and hotels to instant rice and vacuum cleaners. All of the new ventures failed. By 1965, the stock had fallen from 900 to 60 Yen.

Deus Ex Machinas

The end seemed looming, until they caught a bit of good luck on a Hail-Mary product known as the Ultra-Hand. This extendable hand sold over a million units. It pulled them out of their free fall and brought them back to their status quo.

Within a few years, Nintendo secured the rights to distribute Japan's first in-home gaming console, the Magnavox Odyssey. Leadership realized that electronic gaming was the future of entertainment, which was their original core business, and Nintendo set out on the path to develop their own games and eventually their own console.

By 1975, the transition was complete. Donkey Kong's release ensured that Nintendo would be a force in gaming for years to come. They pushed the envelope further with the development of a hand-held toy known as a Game & Watch, which would evolve over time into the industry-changing Gameboy.

What's interesting is the fact that Nintendo certainly suffered massive bumps and bruises in the gaming world, but they survived when many others didn't. In 1985, Nintendo was fully rewarded for all of their efforts when they took the world by storm by releasing the NES (Nintendo Entertainment Center) and introduced one of the most iconic characters in history, our favorite Italian plumber, Mario.

The company continues to innovate in a fickle and expensive business. The ability to fall down and get back up has almost become a trademark for Nintendo. For example, the failures of the Game Cube and Nintendo Wii U were offset by the success of Pokemon GO and the Switch platforms. The company doesn't fold or panic, it regroups and innovates. One thing is for sure. Nintendo is playing for keeps. With over eight billion dollars in cash reserves, *they could run at a loss and still stay in business for the next 38 years.*

A century of failing has created a company that aggressively pushes innovation but that can fail a particular attempt—without destroying the company.

What Nintendo Says about Your Practice

There are very few choices in life or business with zero downside. However, that's what practice owners tend to seek. They want safe bets, a guaranteed ROI, no chance of failure. Our education trained us to fear failure. Failure meant not getting into grad school. It meant not getting into the specialty we wanted. It meant not passing our boards. We have an academic view of failure, not an entrepreneur's view. But the moment you buy a practice, you're no longer in the ivory tower. You're a businessman. Failure has to happen for you to grow. Limiting the downside also leads to limiting the upside. Hospitals and multi-practice conglomerates hire aggressively from outside the field and push new, aggressive business models with Fortune 500 budgets. This paralyzes many owners, but fear has prevented more success than failure ever will.

Where do you start?

A marketing budget is only as good as your marketing.

- Collect data on your campaigns.
- Dig into your practice management software and see which patients are your most profitable. Market to those demographics.
- Read business and marketing articles on a regular basis, and talk to your marketing firm about what you're seeing and how it relates to your particular practice.
- If this sort of thing makes your skin crawl, find a member of your team or even of your family who loves the stuff, and delegate to them.

Look into your patient retention program. Nintendo can afford to innovate because it has enough success to keep running even if new ideas fail. Your "past products" are your current patients. How do you keep them active, engaged in your practice, and ready to refer new patients?

Do you have an R&D budget? What new technologies or services are you planning on adding? What new markets do you hope to attract? What is your investment in CE? Are you and your team only learning the bare minimum to stay licensed, or do you have a growth mindset?

- Learn new procedures, offer new services.
- Have room in the budget so that you can move on from failure while you look for the new service that will set you off from competitors in your region.
- Do you have ideas about how to make your specialty better? Write papers, and connect with people who can help you develop, test, and pilot new treatments and procedures. The minute you stop growing and thinking about improving your

practice and your specialty is the minute you've become a prisoner of your practice, serving your time until retirement.

Nintendo engineers are active, engaged, and constantly coming up with new ideas. For instance, Pokemon GO is a runaway success that grew out of a desire to combine gaming with social connections and exercise. It's the latest stage in a line of thinking that began with sweaty, sock-clad feet pounding through track and field events on the Nintendo Powerpad. As a practice owner, you need to think like an engineer sometimes. What do your patients and potential patients need? How can you create a product or service that will fill that need in an appealing way? Once you have that product, how can you tell them about it? When you start looking at the puzzle of practice growth through the Nintendo lens, you're ready for the challenges of today and the changes of the future.

COURSE 21

Having Trouble with Case Acceptance? The Mona Lisa Can Help

"Don't it always seem to go
That you don't know what you've got til its gone
They paved paradise
And put up a parking lot."

—Joni Mitchell

Big Yellow Taxi is a classic song, and it has a lot to say about how we approach art, and patient care. On August 21st, 1911, an Italian thief named Vincenzo Peruggia stole the Mona Lisa right off the walls of the Louvre. The crime was a media sensation. Rapid access to international news was still relatively new, and this was a story that captured imaginations around the world. Images of the stolen painting appeared in papers across Europe, the US, and even Asia. It took authorities two years to recover the painting. In the meantime, something interesting happened. The museum noticed that more people showed up to see where the painting *used* to be than had come to see the actual painting.

The theft, and resulting publicity, created a legend. Today more than six million visitors a year travel to view the once-missing lady. Most people have no idea how the painting gained its fame. They don't know that for 408 years it was simply regarded as a nice piece from a famous artist. All they know is that it's priceless, it's famous, and they need to see it.

The Mona Lisa's path to fame is an illustration of human nature at work. We are naturally loss averse. We value things more when we think that we're in danger of losing them.

Specialists see this all the time. In my own field, someone who's neglected their teeth for years comes face-to-face with the reality of losing a tooth, and we watch the shock and disbelief wash over their face. How can the patient act surprised? Where was all this concern during the years we watched those pearly whites dull into a dingy greyish brown?

An optometrist often encounters someone who neglected eye exams for years only to suddenly discover that their vision has been damaged by glaucoma. If they'd come in on schedule and been proactive, they could have prevented the loss. How many dermatology patients wait to come in about a skin condition until there's serious scarring? How many cosmetic surgery patients only consider surgery once they've been passed up for multiple promotions? People often need to experience loss before they'll take their own health seriously, and that's a tragedy.

As doctors, we hate to see illness. We hate preventable loss. We want to find a better way to communicate with our patients so that they'll be proactive about protecting their physical and mental well-being. What are our options? Just scare tactics? There's no real way to "create value", as they say. However, we can create better communication tools to give patients perspective and help them understand the reality of their situation. Good scripts can help patients understand what they're in danger of losing and activate the loss aversion instinct so that they're willing to make difficult but necessary changes in their lives.

Dr. John Kois, DMD MSD, runs an evidence-based training center for dental surgeons. He once posed a question to his lecture audience. He asked them how much wear the average person should experience on their teeth in a given year. What's normal? The answer was 11 microns. Now, to the average dental patient that doesn't mean a thing, so he put it into perspective. He said that would mean that the teeth should wear about 1mm for every 100 years. Now that's a number that patients can understand, if you frame it with the right script.

"Mrs. Jones, I know we've talked about a night-guard a few times, but did you realize you have around 200 years (2mm) of wear on these teeth? Most buildings don't last that long. I think it's time to protect them so that they don't chip or decay. "

This script isn't pushy, it isn't sale-sy. It simply adds a new level of perspective. It truthfully establishes the urgency of the situation and should help the patient understand that they're going to lose what they have. Once they grasp that fact, loss aversion will help them make the rational choice.

Create similar scripts for the issues you see in your practice. A patient with high eye pressures who's rejecting medication? Someone putting off surgery for a skin condition? A person losing hours of healthy sleep because their nose can't carry air effectively? Every day you see patients who are in danger of losing the good they have because they avoid treatment. Put the impending loss in clear, objective terms, so that they can understand the risk.

Here's a little worksheet to help you develop scripts for the issues you encounter most often in your own specialty:

Problem:

Normal for a Person this Age is:

Patient's Current Measurement is:

Compared to normal, it matches what you'd expect to see in someone X years old:

At the current rate, function will be lost in X years:

Recommended treatment to halt or reverse damage:

Years gained from treatment:

Your math doesn't have to be exact. Just quick calculations to make the point that the situation is much worse than the average person's and unlikely to improve. The key is to bring home what has been lost and create the desire to preserve what's left.

People care about the Mona Lisa's smile because they nearly lost it. Today, tourists plan entire trips around seeing it. If you can create scripts that help your patients understand how close they are to losing the things they care most about, they'll learn to value them as we value Leonardo's painting.

COURSE 22

An Ancient Roman Lesson on Balance Sheets and Freedom

"Debt is the slavery of the free."

—Publilius Syrus

The Ancient Romans had slaves. Lots of slaves. The whole society depended on slavery. For a freeman, nothing was worse than to lose freedom and become a slave. You lost your ability to choose, to chart your course, to participate in society. Publilius Syrus understood that not all chains are literal ones. A man deep in debt also had no choices and no freedom. His life was consumed by paying off the balance. He couldn't grow or move on or be truly free while he was a debtor.

Most of us started our career in debt. We have medical debt, mortgages, debt from buying our practices. Loans are just the cost of living in the USA in the twenty-first century. Debt is no longer shameful, but it does limit us and chain us down. Today, you're going to learn about a simple tool that will help you get out of debt and live the life Publilius Syrus would have wanted you to. It's called a balance sheet.

What is a balance sheet? It's a statement of the assets, liabilities, and capital of a business or other organization at a particular point in time, detailing the balance of income and expenditure over the preceding period. It is also a powerful tool for managing debt.

Debt Matters

There is good debt and bad debt. Bad debt is debt incurred to buy time or perpetuate the status quo. Good debt is debt that might create production leverage. Maybe you own a pizza parlor and your current oven can produce 10 pizzas an hour, but your wait times are too long for potential customers and you're losing business. Good debt would be purchasing a new or second oven that will increase your production capacity and potentially provide a tax benefit. Bad debt would be financing a new carpet, or maybe a brand-new billboard to advertise your restaurant, which already can't meet demand.

Depending on your business's level of sophistication, borrowing money may actually be a better option than using cash on hand. Apple notoriously has over $80 billion sitting overseas. In 2017, the company sold $7 billion in bonds to fund a stock buyback. Why? Because the interest on the bonds is cheaper than the taxes they'd have to pay to repatriate the overseas monies.

Beyond P&L for Better Debt Management

When it comes to finance, the profit and loss statement (P&L) gets a lot of attention. This document helps explain the path of every dollar that comes in your office. It's like the Plinko board of business. A dollar goes in the top and hopefully something comes out at the bottom. We call the dollars that come out profits, and we want to see lots of them.

The problem is that the P&L often becomes the only financial instrument we use to measure success. Now, most of us don't have accounting degrees, so I can appreciate the natural apprehension about exploring other tools. However, a balance sheet is just as simple as P&L, and it lets you look at your practice and plan your future from a new angle. The balance sheet is all about using ratios to determine the health of your business.

Ratios

You should review your balance sheet once a quarter and rather than just scanning it, there are a couple of simple calculations we can use to get some amazing insight into the health of the business. Let's examine just a few.

To keep us all on the same page, we're going to use this sample balance sheet:

Liquidity ratios measure the ability of the business to pay short term debt, which is any debt that should be paid off within 12 months. There are several different types of liquidity ratios. We'll talk about two of them: the Current Ratio and the Acid Test.

Current Ratio

Also known as the working capital ratio, it is simply found by taking the Current Assets/Current Liabilities. The higher the number, the better.

Dr. Smith Balance Sheet
BALANCE SHEET

ASSETS

CURRENT ASSETS	2016	2015
Cash in bank	$14,000.00	$12,000.00
Accounts receivable	$30,000.00	$18,000.00
Inventory	$5,000.00	$3,000.00
Prepaid expenses	$1,000.00	$2,000.00
Other current assets		
TOTAL CURRENT ASSETS	$50,000.00	$35,000.00

FIXED ASSETS	2016	2015
Machinery and equipment	$50,000.00	$20,000.00
Building	$120,000.00	$100,000.00
Land and buildings	$150,000.00	$100,000.00
Less: Accumulated Depreciation	$25,000.00	$20,000.00
TOTAL FIXED ASSETS (NET OF DEPRECIATION)	$295,000.00	$200,000.00

TOTAL ASSETS	$345,000.00	$235,000.00

LIABILITIES AND EQUITY

CURRENT LIABILITIES	2016	2015
Current Portion of LTD	$7,000.00	$5,000.00
Accounts Payable	$15,000.00	$11,000.00
Notes, short-term (due within 12 months)	$12,000.00	$9,000.00
TOTAL CURRENT LIABILITIES	$34,000.00	$25,000.00

LONG-TERM DEBT	2016	2015
Long term debt	$200,000.00	$150,000.00
TOTAL LONG-TERM DEBT	$200,000.00	$150,000.00

TOTAL LIABILITIES	$234,000.00	$175,000.00

ASSETS AND LIABILITIES

OWNERS' EQUITY	2016	2015
Common Stock	$40,000.00	$25,000.00
Paid in Capitol in excess of par	$22,000.00	$5,000.00
Retained earnings - current	$49,000.00	$30,000.00
TOTAL OWNERS' EQUITY	$111,000.00	$60,000.00

TOTAL LIABILITIES AND EQUITY	$345,000.00	$235,000.00

From our Balance Sheet

- 2016 Current Ratio = 50,000/34,000 = 1.47
- 2015 Current Ratio = 35,000/25,000 = 1.4

This means for every \$1.00 in current 2016 liabilities, they have \$1.47 to cover it. The industry average is \$1.15. The most important thing to remember is to track the ratios over time and watch the trends.

Acid Test

Settle down hippies, this is also called the "Quick Ratio," and it's literally the same equation minus the inventory and prepaid accounts.

Acid Test = (Cash Equivalents + Marketable Securities + Net Receivables)/Current Liabilities

From our Balance Sheet:

- 2016 Acid Test = (14,000 + 30,000)/34,000 = 1.29
- 2015 Acid Test = (12,000 + 18,000)/25,000 = 1.2

If the difference between the current ratio and the acid test is significant, it could point to a bloated inventory. The logic behind the Acid Test is simple. If you needed cash tomorrow, what's the likelihood you could sell your cotton rolls to drum up some cash? Yeah, not gonna happen. So, this tends to be a slightly clearer picture of your actual financial position.

Long Term Debt Ratio (LTD)

This is the measure of the business's ability to handle and meet long term debt obligations. Those are debts being serviced beyond 12 months.

From our Balance Sheet

- Debt ratio = Total Liabilities/Total Assets
- Debt ratio = 234,000/395,000 = 59.24%

This means that 59.24% of our assets are financed by the liabilities. The higher the number, the worse shape you're in.

There are many ways that your balance sheet can be helpful, and this list of ratios is by no means exhaustive, but it's a great place to start. These trends can be a wonderful predictor of tough times ahead, or a great sign that you're on the right track. Servicing debt isn't sexy or fun, but establishing that trend builds momentum, and that gets addictive. These numbers get fun and you'll be amazed how much your bank account will reflect positive shifts, and I don't just mean mathematically.

It doesn't matter where you start, it only matters *that* you start. I recommend that you start today, so that you can have the freedom to expand your practice, innovate, and achieve your goals.

COURSE 23

Growth, Profits, and Amazon's Primacy

Amazon.com, Inc (AMZN) was founded by Jeff Bezos on July 5, 1994. Originally named Cadabra, the company's original purpose was simply to find a better way to sell books. Founder and CEO Jeff Bezos left a lucrative position as a Wall Street hedge fund manager. With degrees from Princeton in computer science and electrical engineering, Bezos had been the youngest Senior Vice President in the history of investment bank D.E. Shaw and Co. Now, he was on his own and ready to use his skills to change the world.

The first Amazon office was his garage. Bezos and a handful of employees built the platform and sold their first book in July of 1995. Being open 24 hours and offering competitive pricing combined with a wide selection led to very rapid growth. People could use Amazon to find books they would never be able to find at their local stores, and the online search was more efficient than combing through paper catalogues and placing many small orders with various tiny retailers.

On May 15th, 1997, Amazon went public. They listed on the Nasdaq under the ticker symbol AMZN. Adding music in 1998 and an online auction element in 1999 was the beginning of what would be become an unstoppable pattern for growth. Instead of trying to eliminate competition, Bezos encouraged large book stores to sell their books through Amazon to reach more people.

This model took the company from $510,000 in 1995 to $19.1 billion in 2008. It was about this time that Amazon began to diversify its offerings. They began to produce physical products like the Kindle as well as virtual services like Amazon Web Services and cloud computing systems.

While Amazon revenues have always been strong, Amazon profits have not. At the time they listed on the Nasdaq, Amazon was losing money and had a valuation of only $438 million. It wasn't until 2001 that Amazon actually turned a profit. By 2016, Amazon had reached $136 billion in revenue. It took them 18 years to match the market capitalization of Walmart, but barely 24 months to double it. Investors believe in this company. Amazon currently has a mind boggling P/E ratio of 630:1 or 243%. Investors don't care, and the stock continues to rise.

While the growth is amazing, the profits are not. If you added up all the profits Amazon has banked, it still wouldn't even match the profits Exxon Mobile makes in 2.5 weeks. The profit margin, by design, is around 1%. The model depends 100% on market share and innovation to grow.

They're certainly on track. Amazon is the juggernaut of ecommerce. Boasting a 30% market share, Amazon has evolved into the one-click source for everything from dog food to original television and movie production. Amazon gained notoriety and legitimacy in the entertainment market after winning numerous awards, included a Golden Globe for *The Marvelous Mrs. Maisel.*

If analysts are correct, Amazon could hit a 50% market share by 2021. Bezos based the company culture on one goal. Raving fans. They rely on repeat business, customer loyalty, and the fact that, for many Americans, ordering online is efficient while traveling to and from the store is not.

What Amazon Can Teach You About Growth and Profits

Amazon may not post huge profits for shareholders to enjoy, but the 1% profits have made Bezos one of the wealthiest men in the world, in spite of his modest $82K salary. (Way to dodge payroll and income taxes, Bezos.) One percent of a gigantic, thriving company that keeps innovating is worth more than a higher percentage in profits from a much smaller company.

So, one of the big lessons from Amazon is: **It pays to innovate and grow.** Amazon reinvests its earnings and is willing to take risks. The Kindle Fire and the associated media has been huge. The Amazon Fire Phone? A bad choice. Amazon Now and Amazon Fresh are taking off. The Whole Foods investment? Looks like it may work out. The Washington Post? Well, everyone needs an expensive hobby, right? Amazon is big enough to try new things and fail.

For you, this means growing your practice enough that you can learn new skills, add new team members, or add locations and hours without worrying that failure will bankrupt you. If you're not trying to grow, you'll never have the room in your budget to try new things, since staff, benefits, materials, and utilities get more expensive every year.

Another lesson from Amazon is: **Be indispensable to your customers.** Once someone has tried Prime, they're not going back. Friends who've used Amazon Fresh and Amazon Now can't bear to give up the easy delivery and freedom from errands. Amazon TV shows keep viewers coming back for more. Kindles become a necessity once you see how they improve your life.

For you, this means be Amazon for your patients. Give them a level of care, service, and appreciation that makes them *unable* to leave you for a competitor. For instance, block your schedule in ways that allow for emergency appointments. "Dr. Jones saw me right away when I had an emergency," makes for a life-long fan. Be accessible. Give them a Keurig and some cake in the waiting room so that they feel pampered and treasured.

Finally, a key lesson is: **Don't throw good money after bad.** No one remembers the Amazon phone anymore; meanwhile Alexa is becoming a household necessity. Amazon knows when to drop a useless product or service so that they can use those resources for something new.

For you, this means asking if you've invested in tech that you never use, and that's now cluttering up your office. Sell it, even at a loss. The failed experiment is keeping you from trying something new *and* making it harder to work. Do you have contracts for various services, from cleaning to IT support? Review them regularly. If you're not getting a good return on your investment, take bids and find someone better. Don't let inertia keep you from improving. Try to review contracts on a three-year cycle. That's generally enough time to tell whether you're happy with someone, and whether you can get a better deal elsewhere.

Finally: **Have fun.** Bezos can continue to grow Amazon because he relishes the challenge of spotting a new need or market, breaking in, and dominating. Treat practice growth like a hobby or a sport. Set goals, and challenge yourself to meet them as quickly as possible. You'll transform your practice and enjoy yourself in the process.

COURSE 24

Blocking for Production instead of Time: The Theory and the Practice

Are you running a busy practice, but feel like you never get ahead? Do you frequently run behind schedule? Do you work your fingers to the bone all day, every day, and yet, when you run the numbers, you're not as successful as your competitors?

Now, it could be that you offer the wrong services or attract the wrong kinds of patients. But it's more likely that your problem is actually one of scheduling and blocking. Most practitioners begin their careers planning their schedules with an eye to annual or monthly production. Then they try to pack every hour with patients and procedures to hit those goals. They see a lot of people for small things—check-ups, emergencies, medication adjustments, etc.—and then jampack their days with these short appointments.

This sets up an unsustainable balance. If even one of these short appointments runs a few minutes over, the whole day is off schedule. And if one insurer cuts reimbursement even a tiny bit on each small visit, the entire budget is blown. Scheduling this way is stressful, exhausting, and unfulfilling. There's a better way. One of the best scheduling philosophies I have ever seen comes from the Productive Dentist Academy.

Hourly Production Gives You Breathing Room

So, how does planning for hourly production give you more breathing room? The key is to block appointments by what they produce, not by how much time they take. Under the old system, if two appointments took the same amount of time, you blocked them in the schedule the same way. So the one-hour $200 procedure and the one-hour $1200 procedure each took up one hour in your schedule.

With hourly production, that changes. So imagine a small practice aiming for $1,000,000 in production. They're open 48 weeks a year and 35 hours a week. To hit their production goals for the year, that means their hourly production should be around $600 an hour. If they only have two operatories, they literally can't hit that goal doing $200 an hour appointments. That, right there, is important information. Suddenly they realize that they need to schedule more high-value procedures.

Now, look at that $1200, one-hour procedure. To schedule for hourly productivity, block it in as a two-hour procedure. Now the hourly goals for those two hours have been met. You can use the other operatory for whatever you want: post-procedure appointments, check-ups, imaging, medication adjustments, or even seeing emergencies. It doesn't matter.

With the extra hour in the first operatory, you can see an emergency patient, if you have time when the procedure is done. You can see patients more quickly and shorten wait times. You can head to your office and spend some time on professional reading and business planning so you can expand the practice, or, heck, you can even take a nap. It doesn't matter. You're covered for the entire two hours.

So, how do you do this in practice?

- Calculate your desired hourly production by taking your annual production and dividing by the numbers you're open each year.
- Start blocking based on that number. If you aim for $1000/hour and you have a $6000 procedure, then 6 hours of that operatory are blocked out.
- Educate your scheduling staff so that they respect the blocks. No squeezing people in.
- When you're scheduling several months in advance, it helps to have one operatory reserved for major procedures—those that represent two or more hours of your goal being met.
- Resist the urge to fill those blocks with less productive appointments. Your patients who need major procedures deserve to be seen promptly.
- If those blocks aren't being filled, it's time to look at your marketing, consultations, case presentations, and financing. Do not be embarrassed to focus your efforts on these bigger appointments. Meeting your hourly goals is what gives you the freedom to help more people and see more patients.
- If, at some point, you find yourself meeting your hourly production goals effortlessly, it's time to up the goals and find ways to take your practice to the next level.

What If You Can't Meet Your Goals?

When I recommend that someone make the switch to hourly production, this is usually the biggest question. What if you can't make your goals?

There are a couple of reasons why a practice might not be able to hit its hourly production goals:

1 **The goals were too ambitious.** If you're in a suburb or metro area, this is unlikely. But if your practice is in an isolated rural area, maybe there just aren't enough people to meet your goals.

   What to do about it: If this is the case, you have a few options. You can aim for a lower goal. You can move to a more profitable region. Or, you can cast a wider net with your marketing, and offer services, financing, and a customer experience that draws patients from a larger area. The right option for you depends on your personal financial and lifestyle goals, your attachment to the community, and your willingness to stretch in new directions.

2 **Your team isn't respecting the blocks.** In many practices, it's a struggle to get schedulers to respect the blocks. If a block is still empty a month or three weeks out, they fill it up with low-value appointments. Then any high value procedures that come up in the intervening time get pushed to later start dates, and you start losing patients to doctors who can get them in sooner.

   What to do about it: If this is happening, retrain the team. Issue reminders. If possible, have your IT staff make it impossible to override the blocks until the day before. For scheduling for hourly production to work, you have to leave space for your most productive appointments.

3 **You are not attracting enough high-value appointments to your office.** The people who need these high-value procedures are out there, they're just not coming to you for them.

What to do about it: It's time to take stock and figure out *why* you're not attracting them.

- **Internal Marketing:** Are you advertising these services to existing patients and staff? Are you asking for referrals and following through on them?
- **External Marketing:** Have you advertised on social media, using Google AdWords, or in local wedding and prom publications? What is your website like? Does it promote high value procedures, or is it generic? What about your web address? Is it memorable and related to the work you want to be doing?
- **Consultations:** If someone calls for a consultation, how quickly can you get them in? Next day or at least the same week is ideal. If they have to wait, they'll give up or go elsewhere.
- **Case Presentations:** Do you need to work on your case presentation skills, so patients choose the best option for their situation?
- **Financing Options:** Are you offering easy monthly payments with interest? Or are you turning away payment-worthy patients with bad credit? What can you do to make it easier for your patients to accept treatment?
- **Scheduling:** How easy is it for patients to schedule this procedure? How many follow-ups are there? How much lost work? Is there a way to ease the time constraints to get more people in?

- **Service Mix:** Is there too much competition for the procedures you offer? What new, high-value services can you offer that will set you apart from the crowd and help you open new markets?

Take the time to analyze your hourly production and to make and reach new goals on a regular basis. Once your practice is thriving, you'll have the time and financial freedom you need to truly enjoy your work.

COURSE 25

Philanthropy Works in Both Directions

Most of these mini-courses have been focused on business, financial, and personal growth, but it's time to take a look at another key element of having a really great practice and a really great life. How are you giving back to the community?

Remember, we learned that *Success is as success does.* Well, one thing success does, again and again, is try to give back and make the world a better place. Look at Bill Gates. He doesn't just kick back and relax in retirement. He's devoted his talents and resources to improving health and education around the world. Many people in your field spend time working in charity clinics or on medical missions. For people who have money, but not time, there are youth centers to fund, local charities, and people in need around the globe.

Why does success in business lead to philanthropy? Why does philanthropy, in turn, lead to more success in business? I could go into some long-winded spiritual explanation about karma, or say that what goes around comes around, but it's really simpler than that.

Philanthropy is part of human nature, and if you deny this part of yourself, you won't be happy in the long-term.

Think about how you feel when you help someone regain their health, coach a winning team, teach a child to ride a bike, or give to a worthy cause. You feel good. Most of us are hardwired to help others, to enjoy giving gifts, and to want to see positive change in the lives of those around us.

The problem is that when you're stuck in a maelstrom of paying off loans and building a business—often while simultaneously building a family—it's easy to get bogged down and feel like you don't have the time or resources to do anything but focus on salary and work. And when that happens, your joy slowly beings to slip away until everything is a rat race and nothing is fun anymore.

It's time to be intentional about giving back to the community. The question is, what form of giving will suit you best?

If you don't have much disposable income at the moment, but have a lot of time outside of work... Consider volunteering with a community clinic or free medical service program in your area. Many states and counties have charities devoted to running a clinic once a month or once a year. If there's not one in your immediate area, check with regional medical schools. There will be somewhere where you can use your talents to help America's neediest people and really change lives.

If you want to prioritize time with your kids... You have control over your schedule, since you own the practice. Make time to coach, to lead a scout troop, or to volunteer at their schools. Get out there and into the community. Enjoy your children while meeting your neighbors. In today's world, parent volunteers are in short supply. Giving your time means that there will be activities for kids from all walks of life to enjoy. And if you've never coached or led a scouting group, don't worry. You'll learn quickly, and your kids will love knowing that you care enough to try.

If you have no time and no disposable income... Take on some charity cases in your office. Let deserving patients receive care at cost, or forgive balances for holidays. You'll make a huge difference in their lives, and if you're doing well with your hourly production, you have time to use that other operatory for charity work.

If you'd like to concentrate your giving in a short period of time, such as your vacation... The world needs medical missionaries. So many people in the developing world die or suffer permanent disability from ailments that we treat routinely in the United States. Find a program that matches your skills, and prepare to work harder, and change more lives, than you ever have before.

If you have money, but no time... Find a cause you're passionate about and support it at a high level. Does your local YMCA need a new pool? Is there a scholarship you'd like to fund? Contact a local organization and see what they need, or go through your area's Community Foundation. Use your giving to create a positive difference, either in your own community or abroad.

Not Just Good for the Soul, also Good for the Business

Giving back can help you reconnect with your community, your family, and the reasons you decided to practice medicine. And that, in turn, can actually help your business do better. When you volunteer and engage with the community, you:

- Learn more about what the people in your area need and want from your practice;
- Become a familiar and well-liked figure;
- Earn the trust of those around you, as they see that you are reliable and compassionate;
- Help give your team pride in the practice, so that they're happier and more engaged;
- Form deeper bonds with your patients, so that they become raving fans;
- Get the energy you need to reinvest yourself in your work;
- Start a cycle. Doing good in the community results in your practice doing good, which gives you more ability to do good in the community.

Your work and your world can't be in isolation from each other. Your practice can serve as the engine that fuels your philanthropy and volunteerism and your philanthropy and volunteerism fuel your practice. It's a single ecosystem, and both parts need to be there in order for you to truly love your job and your life.

So, ask yourself today: What resources do I have that I can use to serve others? Who needs my help? What sort of work would I enjoy doing? What organizations really impress me?

Now, go out there, make some calls, and get started Doing Good by Doing Good.

COURSE 26

Monthly Meetings that Don't Suck

If you want to transform your practice, the place to start is your monthly team training. "Wait," I can hear some of you say, "What do you mean, a monthly team training?" If you don't already have a once-a-month training for your team, go and put one on the calendar right now. I'll wait. I'll explain how you're going to run it once you get back from scheduling it.

A monthly team training isn't the same as an in-service day or continuing education (CE). Those things are important, but most practices already have those down. If you have a new practice management system or there are new rules or regulations coming into effect, you hire a consultant, close the office for the day, and let someone else train your team and bring them up to speed.

The monthly training isn't for big changes. It's not for directives from on high. It's for things that you and senior team members have noticed that need more work, but which don't need a whole day with PowerPoints and notebooks and quizzes. Your monthly training is going to be about an hour long, on the same day every month. Ideally, it should happen either an hour before the practice opens in the morning, or over a lunch out. Provide a good meal and 99% of your staff grumbles will be silenced. Anyone can endure an hour of training if there's good food involved. Some months, you'll train the whole team for an hour. Other months, the training will be a brief introduction followed by breakout sessions where clinical staff, front office, billing, and scheduling can all work on their own trainings. It depends on what you need in a given month.

I like to come up with training ideas by watching my teams, seeing where they encounter snafus or where the patients aren't moving through the practice completely smoothly, and then I target interventions for small, specific problems. You may want to come up with a curriculum for a year's worth of trainings, or even survey your team to see what they'd like to know more about. See what works for your practice. Just make sure that the once-a-month training is on the calendar and happens every month. In the absence of trainings like this, bad habits get ingrained, new team members take longer to learn the ropes, and tensions rise. So commit to the monthly trainings.

If you aren't sure what topics to cover with the team, here are a few key ones that every office on the planet needs to review. It doesn't matter whether you're the top-grossing office in your region or a new practice just starting up. These are areas where everyone's team can and should improve, and where an hour of training can lead to big rewards:

1 **Phone Skills.** How quickly do you answer the phone? Can the back office step in when the front office is overwhelmed? How do you overcome objections and get patients in for

the initial consultation? Since the phone is often a patient's first contact with the office, how do you make that first call amazing for them? And, from the technology side, how do you handle holds and transfers to make them as seamless and painless as possible? How can you use technology to rectify missed calls?

2 **Total Body Health.** Yes, we're a specialty office, but we also recognize that all of the body's systems affect each other, and we want our patients to be in the best possible health. How can all of us, from the front desk to the clinical staff to the billing department, encourage good habits and pro-active behaviors in our patients? What can we do to make educating them about health an easier and more effective process?

3 **Positive Feedback 101.** When you see one of your team-mates make a mistake, how do you react? What effect do negative interactions have on the atmosphere of the office as a whole? Here's a chance to practice offering correction, education, and encouragement in ways that make the whole team stronger and the whole office a better medical home for our patients!

4 **Mission Statement Refresher Course.** Do you remember what our practice mission statement is? Is it a good mission statement? How could it be improved? What can you, personally, do in your job to put the mission statement into practice on a daily basis? What can we do so that our patients see that our mission is more than just some words on the wall? Think about times you've had to make a decision quickly in the practice. How can the mission statement guide decision making and keep everyone on the same page so that our patients get a cohesive customer experience?

5 **When and How to ask for Referrals and Reviews.** Referrals and Reviews are the quickest and easiest way to build up the practice. But when do you ask for them? Which team members are best at asking? What technologies do we have to help with referrals and reviews? How can we create a routine to get more, and better, referrals and reviews? What is our goal for referrals and reviews for the next six months, and how can we reach it?

6 **A Patient's Eye View of the Practice.** Walk through the practice from the waiting room to checkout just as a patient would. How can we make their journey easier and more pleasant? What bottlenecks have various departments noticed? How can we relieve them to minimize wait times and maximize patient comfort?

7 **Internal Marketing 101.** The doctor isn't the only one who helps persuade a patient to investigate a helpful procedure. How does each member of the practice help educate and inform patients about our services? What can we do to make this role easier for everyone?

By the time you've had monthly, one-hour meetings on each of these seven topics, you'll have probably collected ideas of your own for future trainings. For a monthly meeting, keep it brief, to the point, and positive. Remember, it's always easier for your team to replace a negative behavior with a positive one than to simply avoid the negative behavior with no replacement offered.

Sample Schedule for Training

7:00 am. Meet, get breakfast, sit down.

7:05 am. A brief introduction to the problem, with specific examples.

7:10 am. What other examples have you seen of this issue? Discuss.

7:15 am. What solutions do you think would help us improve on this issue? Take suggestions on the whiteboard, discuss.

7:30 am. Try out scripts to help navigate the issue. These can be preplanned or come out of the discussion. Do what works best for your practice, or vary it depending on the issue.

7:45 am. Front office staff leaves to open up the front office; Doctor gives goals for improvement and a timeline; two months is good. Hang a goal tracker sheet in the staff room, so everyone can see the practice's progress towards the goals.

8:00 am. Everyone starts their day.

Remember, these trainings are short, targeted, and about working as a team to improve the practice and reach goals, not shaming people who've made mistakes. Make sure every training ends with a positive action that your team members can take, and an achievable goal for improvement. By focusing on these sorts of practice issues once a month, you can create a culture of continuous improvement that puts your practice at the top.

COURSE 27

The Secret to Unruly Team Member Self-Correction

"It's very important to have a feedback loop, where you're constantly thinking about what you've done and how you could be doing it better."

—Elon Musk

Imagine you're at work, moving between patient exam rooms, and you see an employee in the corridor doing something wrong. Maybe they're not following a checklist that you've put in place. Maybe they've answered the phone, but not in the on-brand way for your office. Maybe, heaven forbid, they're being snippy with one of your new patients. It's the middle of the day, you have patients waiting, but you really can't let these kinds of behaviors go, can you?

So what do you do? Your first option is to correct the person, firmly and quickly, right there, in front of everyone else. On the one hand, that deals with the problem so you don't have to think about it anymore. On the other hand, it shames your employee in front of other people and patients, rebukes them without any actual remediation, and injures your relationship with that employee. If the mistake is a truly dangerous one and immediately life-threatening, then this is your only option. However, if the employee error is annoying or off-brand but not dangerous, correction can wait until later. Make sure you have well-defined job descriptions and your team members are fully aware what duties are their responsibility. You cannot get mad if someone legitimately does not know what they don't know.

So, how do you give feedback in a way that is helpful, team-building, and ultimately teaches rather than shames? I'm going to let you in on a little secret...let your team member do it for themselves. Remember the chapter about motivational interviewing? We take those concepts and apply them to an underachieving team member, in a way that brings to light what is going on and how it is impacting the business. Here is how it works.

Have a private meeting with the team member. That alone will let them know something is up, and chances are good they already know what it is you are going to address. If they know what is expected of them, they know when they aren't meeting the expectation. This meeting won't be a surprise. Here are a series of questions that will help you achieve the best change in your employee.

"Why do you think I need to talk to you today?" When they answer, they will be defining the issue, not you. This is key. When they hear themselves say what the issue is, you are no longer the bad guy telling them what is wrong. If they truly don't know what is going on, go ahead and tell them.

“How do you think this <problem> affects <me, the business>?” Let them define the negative outcome of their behavior.

“What are some ways we can make sure <this problem> does not happen again?” At this point they will come up with their own action plan to stop the behavior.

“How long will it take to implement these changes?” They establish the timeline for when you can expect the behavior to change.

“How will we know if those changes are working?” Here they define the intended outcome.

“What should happen if things don’t change?” They will supply the course of corrective action here. Again, no being the bad guy. They are telling you what should happen if they don’t meet their own expectation.

At this point, write out the action plan based on their answers. Both parties sign and date it, and decide on when the next meeting should be to check progress.

Motivational Interviewing is a powerful way to take a bad behavior and turn it into an opportunity for the employee or team member to self-reflect and define their own course of corrective action.

If You Are Being the Bad Guy

If you find that you can’t seem to hold your temper and deliver correction calmly, it may be that you’re the one who needs more training, scripts, and practice. As the business owner, you’re part visionary, part innovator, and part mentor. If you’re weak on the mentoring side of things, get training and get help. Your practice will grow more quickly and function better if you can create the support team that you need—developing the staff you have is nearly always less expensive than hiring experienced people away from somewhere else.

COURSE 28

Change is Hard.

So you want to make a change in the practice. Maybe you plan on changing your hours. Maybe you're excited about adding a new service to the mix. Maybe you've decided it's time to change up the employee bonus structure; you want to restructure the organizational chart; or you're bringing in a new IT product. It doesn't matter. Change is hard, and there are bound to be members of your team who are opposed to the changes.

People like being comfortable at work. They like knowing what to expect. When you suggest changing anything about the way they do their job, the natural response is panic. "What if it makes my job miserable? What if I can't do it, and I get fired? What if the whole practice goes under? My family will starve!" Change at work affects us on a gut level, because work is how we keep our families fed and sheltered. That means that, whether the changes you're planning are large ones or small ones, you need to get the team on board. If you don't, your attempts at change will fail. You may be the boss, but there are more of them than there are of you.

You also can't simply spring change on people. That feels like an attack. Before you make a big change, you need to lay the groundwork for the change. We often think to do that with IT projects. We warn people that change is coming, enlist their aid in demo-ing new products, hire a consultant to train them, have a phase-in period where people are getting up to speed, and then, finally, shift 100% to the new system. And we still lose some valued team members who just don't want to deal with the change.

When we're putting new systems and procedures in place in other areas, we're a lot less intentional. We're more likely to spring it on our team all at once, and expect instant compliance. After all, it's just a checklist, or a new phone script, or a new way of asking for referrals. It's not something you have to learn, like a computer program, right?

Wrong. Habits are habits. Change is hard even when there aren't logins to remember and menus to navigate. It's time to start treating all changes as if they were the rollout of new IT.

If you're ready to make the changes that will transform your practice, here's how to roll them out. Note: In general, it's better to make, and focus on, one change at a time. Too much at once is disorienting for your staff to put into place and hard for you to track. We're transforming your practice, but a slow rollout that sticks is better than a quick rollout that fails miserably.

So, do you have ideas for a change? Are you shifting to scheduling for hourly production? Let's use that as an example, since it's something you ought to do anyway, no matter what your practice is like.

Three Months ahead of the Rollout

Have a team meeting to explain the issue in terms that make it important to your staff. "Our practice isn't doing as well as it should be, and as a result, it's getting harder to keep up with raises and benefits and other perks. The problem isn't that we need new patients. It's how we schedule those patients. I want to shift to a new kind of scheduling that will help us meet our financial goals for the practice by using our days more effectively. It's not going to mean more work or longer hours. It should actually result in breathing space." Then, explain the change, and give a timeline for the rollout. The reason you need a lag for a scheduling shift is that, if you're like many specialty offices, your schedule is probably full for months ahead. So the change is going to take time since you've already scheduled appointments.

Organize a training on block scheduling for your scheduling staff. Their lives are going to change soonest, because they are going to have to change how they schedule before the rest of the staff experiences the change in the rhythm of the day and appointment flow.

Two Months ahead of the Rollout

Either you, or someone else on the team, should be giving regular updates on the rollout process. Have your schedulers begun using the new blocks for appointments more than three months out? Are you encountering any snags? What is the new schedule going to look like? How does the team need to reorganize to cope with one operatory meeting goals while the other handles low-production procedures?

Now is the time to have either your schedulers, if they're ready, or a professional consultant teach the rest of the team about the new schedule and how it will work. You may want to discuss putting some of your clinical staff in control of scheduling for minor procedures and routine appointments in the second operatory. If something involves very little doctor time, just a quick two-minute check or something, you can safely delegate scheduling to the people who will be doing the bulk of the work. Remember to take details like the availability of imaging equipment into account with these smaller appointments. However, the staff members who deal with these appointments *should* have a better idea of snags and snafus related to that than you do, if you're not a micromanager.

One Month ahead of the Rollout

Training should be complete by now. It's time to come up with some benchmarks and goals, and a system so that the whole team can see how the practice is meeting goals with the new system and analyze where they're falling short and how to improve.

Also, plan a party for immediately after the total rollout. One way to keep staff morale up in times of change is to treat the change as a cause for celebration, not a chore. It can be as simple as a catered breakfast or lunch or even just a cake from the local bakery. The key is to reward your staff for their work up until that point, and to cheer them on as they complete the difficult transition.

Two Weeks ahead of the Rollout

You did it. In two weeks the practice will be working on an hourly production schedule all of the time, from now on. Take time to meet with the team members individually to ask about questions or concerns. This is an important step. It lets you get a team-level view of any looming problems, helps people get a firmer grasp on the change and what it means to them, and gives you the cleanest shot at a smooth transition.

One Week ahead of the Rollout

Put up a countdown in the breakroom, so people can mentally prepare. Have a meeting for one last run-through on the change. Have your schedulers check in with the team, so they can see how another department successfully transitioned. You're prepared for this.

Rollout Day

Announce to the team that the process is complete. Have cake and a little celebration. Be prepared for a few wrinkles in the coming weeks, but know that, with everyone on board, the new process will soon be a comfortable habit, just like the old one was.

This method of achieving buy-in may seem a bit overly detailed, but when you carefully lay the groundwork before a transition, the transition itself becomes easier. Once you've successfully made one change, start planning the next. Eventually, the change process will, itself, become routine, and you'll have a team who can successively adapt and grow as the practice changes.

COURSE 29

Communication with Patients and Team: You've Probably Been Doing It Wrong

As a group, most doctors, in any specialty, are pretty good at school. We got good grades most of our lives. We had excellent test scores. We studied like maniacs to get our degrees and pass our boards. We collect CE credits like kids on Halloween collect candy. We like facts. We like information. We like education.

So, when we're trying to convince a patient to accept a treatment protocol or a staff member to do things in a new way, we tend to try to educate them. Out come the facts. Out come the procedures. Out come the lists and the references and the articles. If we're trying to be exceptionally easygoing, maybe we throw in a video or two, just to make it more like watching TV. Our gut reaction is to communicate to educate. "Surely, if people *know* better, they will *do* better," we tell ourselves. And then we're amazed when the knowledge changes nothing, or when they act like we're irritating and overbearing. What are we doing wrong? Who *doesn't* want information when making decisions?

Take a deep breath. I'm going to tell you a hard truth here. *Most people* don't want facts and information flung at them when they're making decisions. Communicating in this way doesn't help persuade them, it just overwhelms them. Yes, *you* want all the technical specs on something before you buy into it, but that is because *you are weird*. If you weren't weird, you wouldn't be where you are today. In terms of clinical success, it's a good kind of weird. In terms of talking to patients? It's time to learn to talk like a normal human being.

Most people communicate to *connect*, not to educate.

What does this mean? When you come in and start rattling off facts, you don't come across as someone who cares, even though you do care, intensely. You come across as a pompous know-it-all. Your patients, and often your team, don't care that much about the facts. Have you noticed how car commercials tend to focus on feelings about the car, not in-depth technical diagrams? It's the same thing. Feelings move people. Facts are just what they use to justify the decision in retrospect. To get your patients to accept treatment and your team to make changes, you need to communicate with empathy in mind, not information. Save the information for when you're with other education-junkies at a conference or CE class.

Connecting with Patients During Case Presentation

The key to communicating to connect is to let your patient know that 1) you care about them; 2) you have been listening to them; and 3) you can solve their problems.

So, for instance, imagine a patient is a candidate for robot-assisted surgery. If you give in to your natural impulse, you'll be tempted to talk about the robot. Its technical specifications, its capabilities, how small the incisions are, how much better the success rate is. You're excited about the robot. You're enthusiastic about the ways that technology has changed medicine for the better. You want the patient to know how marvelous it is and to understand exactly what the procedure will do.

What the patient hears is "Blah blah blah SURGERY! Pain! Recovery times! Blah blah blah." In their head, it sounds like what you're excited about is their suffering, not the cool robot.

An approach that prioritizes connection looks like this. "Mrs. Smith, I understand that pain has really affected your day to day life. What's been hardest for you? What do you wish you could do?" Then, for instance, if she mentioned her grandchildren, you could continue with, "After this procedure, you should be able to take your grandchildren to the park again, and you won't have to miss another Little League game due to pain. The whole surgery is outpatient, so you can be home the same night. Let me help you get out of pain, so you can be the grandmother you want to be." You can explain what the surgery does, but you don't need to go into great technological detail. Your patient mostly cares about pain levels, recovery time, and improved function.

It doesn't matter how much you care about your patients. When you step into educator mode, what they see is someone lecturing them. In connection mode, they see someone who cares about them and wants to help them achieve their goals. Be a connector, and you have the chance to change more lives.

Is Education Dead?

Now, education has to happen eventually, of course. Your patients need to learn what they need to do to stay healthy, how to prepare for surgery, and how to take care of themselves after a procedure. However, connection comes first.

Good teachers know this. Most students won't learn unless they have a connection with the teacher. The emotional connection needs to proceed the information sharing. Otherwise, the children don't retain the information.

This is why, often, assistants have better luck educating than the doctor does. They see more of the patients and are more likely to engage in small talk about families and hobbies. They seem more like friends, so the patient remembers what they say.

But, when it comes to case presentation, you're the educator and the communicator. So, build that connection first. Deal with the emotional sale before the informational end of things. Let people know how the procedure will make them *feel*; address their hopes and fears; and then get back to the technical stuff. (Which they probably won't remember anyway. Have you ever talked to a non-medically oriented relative about what they *think* the doctor told them at their last appointment? It's hilarious. Luckily, they don't have to remember everything the doctor told them in order to follow through on treatment. They just have to like and trust their doctor.)

Communication for Connection Cheat Sheet

It can be tough to break out of your instinctual communication patterns. I know one person who enters conversations with the mantra "Don't talk about advances in materials science... don't talk about advances in materials science." The only way to improve your communication skills is to *practice.* Practice making small talk. Practice reflecting a patient's feelings back to them. Practice going into a new conversation without the goal of delivering information.

In the meantime, here's a little cheat sheet to help you get started on connecting before educating:

- Start with empathy: a variation on, "I know this condition must really be hurting you mentally and physically."
- Ask a question about what they most hope will change once it is fixed.
- Reflect that answer back to them, affirming that it is a good hope.
- Explain the expected effects of the procedure in general terms: i.e. "This will replace your lens so that you can see clearly again. It will also cure your astigmatism."
- Make the connection to how the change will improve their life. "Afterwards, you'll be able to drive again, and you can make that trip to see your brother that you talked about."
- Close by mentioning how happy it makes you to be able to change lives like this.
- Then, "Would you like to know more about how the procedure works? What questions do you have?"

If someone asks a question about technical details, then give them the information. Just keep in mind, most patients will want to know about preparation, risks, and recovery times. They come to you because they know that you're an expert in your field. They don't need to know everything you know about a procedure, because they trust you to take good care of them. What they most need is reassurance that, yes, you understand that they're trusting you with their lives and that you value them, their goals, and their hopes. If you can communicate that message successfully, you'll persuade more patients to accept treatments, increase compliance with dietary/exercise instructions, and create fans of your practice who can't wait to refer family, friends, and even random strangers to you.

COURSE 30

A Total Practice Inventory

Yes, I know not every month has 31 days. But most do. In lieu of an inspiring conclusion, I give you the Total Practice Inventory. Here's a chance to step back and look at your practice, and your life, in light of the 30 mini-courses you just worked through. Get some paper or a laptop and get to work.

When you're done, circle the three aspects of your practice that you're least happy with. These will be the starting points for your transformation. Once you've improved those areas, move onto the next two or three trouble spots. Plan on doing this inventory once a year. You'll find that there are always ways to tweak your practice, improve its performance, and get closer to your goals for your life and work.

Leadership

- What roles (IT, Collections, Lab) do you currently outsource?
- What roles could be outsourced for a lower cost than they're done in-house?

- What roles do you, personally, fill in the practice?
- Which could be delegated?
- What training does your current team need to take on those roles?
- Who would be a good fit for each role?
- How many times a week do you intervene in situations involving low-level employees?
- What is your three-year plan for the practice?
- What is your mission statement?
- How can you align the two?
- What new business skill will you learn this year?

HR Issues

- When will you next hire a new employee?
- What are your recruitment plans?
- What new areas can you recruit from?
- How do you evaluate employees?
- What can you do to give employees a greater stake in the success of the practice?
- What are your monthly meeting topics for the next six months?
- How often do you correct staff members?
- How often do you compliment staff members?
- What changes are coming to your practice in the next year?
- What is your plan for the rollout?

Case Presentation

- What is your current case acceptance rate?
- What are the most common reasons patients give for rejecting treatment?
- What is one plan you can implement to address the most prominent concern?
- What case presentation scripts do you currently use?
- What new ones do you need to develop and practice?

Service Mix

- How often do you add a new service?
- What was the last service you added?
- What is your most popular service?
- What % of your procedures is it?
- What % of your revenue comes from it?
- What is your most profitable service?
- What % of your procedures is it?
- What % of your revenue comes from it?
- What new service would you like to add?
- What would your ideal service mix be, in percentages?
- What is it now?
- What are the most common diagnoses in your practice?
- What conditions are probably underdiagnosed due to time, patient resistance, or treatment options?
- How can you improve your diagnosis rate?
- What diagnostic tools, assessments, or technologies would you need to add?

Data and Tracking

- What performance metrics do you currently track?
- What areas do you not have the ability to track?
- What metrics would you like to be able to track?
- If you sold your practice today, what would it be worth?
- How can you increase the value?
- Who are your highest value patients?
- What do they have in common?
- What % of your procedures are self-pay?
- What financing can you offer to increase the % of self-pay procedures?
- How much debt does your practice currently have?
- Who holds the notes?
- At what interest rates?
- When will the debt be paid off?
- Would it help to pay it off more quickly?
- Do you use a balance sheet?
- What is your acid test for each of the last five years?
- What is the trend?
- What is your hourly production goal?
- What was your average hourly production last week?

Patient Experience

- What percentage of your appointments begin on time?
- What percentage of your appointments run over?

- Do patients have a way to give feedback on particular team members?
- Which team members do patients connect with the best?
- What is the shabbiest part of the office?
- How can you spruce it up?
- What procedures do you lack patient testimonials and before/after shots for?
- How can you get those testimonials and pictures?
- What % of patients follow through with self-care recommendations?
- What is your goal for % of patients complying with self-care routines?
- What % of active patients from last year are active patients this year?
- What is the average number of years a patient stays with your practice?
- What are the top three reasons patients give for leaving your practice?
- What do you need to do to become irreplaceable and indispensable for your patients?

Marketing

- What mediums will target people like your best patients?
- What are you doing to market to existing patients?
- Where is your internal marketing weakest?
- In what mediums do you currently advertise?
- What advertising medium would you like to try?

Personal Fulfillment

- How often do you get together and talk with other professionals?
- What percentage of your children's games/recitals/performances/award ceremonies do you attend?
- If married, how often do you have a night out with your spouse?
- How often do you socialize with friends?
- What was the last non-working vacation you took?
- How often do you spend time outside during daylight hours?
- What are your hobbies?
- How often can you spend time on your hobbies?
- Where do you volunteer?
- Where do you donate?
- What causes would you *like* to be involved in?

There you have it: a complete inventory. Now you know where you stand in light of this book. So where do you want to be?